GROWING
CARNATIONS
AND PINKS

GROWING
CARNATIONS AND PINKS

FRED C SMITH

SERIES EDITOR
ALAN TOOGOOD

WARD LOCK

A WARD LOCK BOOK

First published in the UK in this edition 1994
by Ward Lock, Villiers House, 41/47 Strand
LONDON WC2N 5JE

A Cassell Imprint

Originally published in the Plantsman's Guides series (1990)

Distributed in the United States
by Sterling Publishing Co., Inc.
387 Park Avenue South, New York,
NY 10016-8810

Distributed in Australia
by Capricorn Link (Australia) Pty Ltd
2/13 Carrington Road, Castle Hill NSW 2154

A British Library Cataloguing in Publication
Data block for this book may be obtained from the British Library

ISBN 0 7063 7262 X

Typeset by Chapterhouse Limited, Formby, England
Printed and bound in Spain by Cronion S.A., Barcelona

CONTENTS

PUBLISHER'S NOTE

Readers are requested to note that in order to make the text intelligible in both hemispheres, plant flowering times, etc. are described in terms of seasons, not months. The following table provides an approximate 'translation' of seasons into months for the two hemispheres.

Northern Hemisphere		Southern Hemisphere
Mid-winter	= January	= Mid-summer
Late winter	= February	= Late summer
Early spring	= March	= Early autumn
Mid-spring	= April	= Mid-autumn
Late spring	= May	= Late autumn
Early summer	= June	= Early winter
Mid-summer	= July	= Mid-winter
Late summer	= August	= Late winter
Early autumn	= September	= Early spring
Mid-autumn	= October	= Mid-spring
Late autumn	= November	= Late spring
Early winter	= December	= Early summer

Captions for colour photographs on chapter-opening pages:

pp. 8–9 Dianthus 'Telstar'. One of the modern pink varieties easily grown from seed.

pp. 16–17 A mixed border with a background of campanulas and other taller plants, with a variety of pink dianthus in the front.

pp. 32–33 A rockery display planted with thyme and dianthus.

pp. 52–53 A typical cottage garden of mixed flowers. The neat grass path is edged with pinks.

pp. 72–73 Dianthus 'Magic Charm' a very good pink variety grown from seed.

pp. 100–101 Dianthus alpinus, a rock pink that makes an excellent show on a rock garden.

pp. 120–121 Border carnations making a grand display along the grass edging.

EDITOR'S FOREWORD

This unique series takes a completely fresh look at the most popular garden and greenhouse plants.

Written by a team of leading specialists, yet suitable for novice and more experienced gardeners alike, the series considers modern uses of the plants, including refreshing ideas for combining them with other garden or greenhouse plants. This should appeal to the more general gardener who, unlike the specialist, does not want to devote a large part of the garden to a particular plant. Many of the planting schemes and modern uses are beautifully illustrated in colour.

The extensive A–Z lists describe in great detail hundreds of the best varieties and species available today.

For the historically-minded, each book opens with a brief history of the subject up to the present day and, as appropriate, looks at the developments by plant breeders.

The books cover all you need to know about growing and propagating. The former embraces such aspects as suitable sites and soils, planting methods, all-year-round care and how to combat pests, diseases and disorders.

Propagation includes raising plants from seeds and by vegetative means, as appropriate.

For each subject there is a society (sometimes more than one), full details of which round off each book.

The plants that make up this series are very popular and examples can be found in many gardens. However, it is hoped that these books will encourage gardeners to try some of the better, or perhaps more unusual, varieties; ensure some stunning plant associations; and result in the plants being grown well.

CHAPTER ONE

PAST AND PRESENT

The genus *Dianthus* encompasses many variations. These are perpetual flowering, spray and border carnations, old fashioned, laced, show, Allwoodii and hybrid, rock and annual pinks, and sweet williams. Whether your interest lies in colour variations, show blooms, or merely in producing a pleasant looking garden to give hours of pleasure while you sit in comfort in your own home, do not hesitate to make a start.

It has given me great pleasure over the last fifty years to grow and show a wide variety of the genus *Dianthus*, helping and advising others to share the enjoyment I have found. Friendships within the gardening fraternity have been established and maintained over many years.

EARLY HISTORY AND DEVELOPMENT

It can be assumed that carnations, earlier known as gilliflowers, were cultivated in many parts of Europe and Asia long before written records were kept. Since their introduction into the British Isles, there has been progressive development in both carnations and pinks. Because, in our society, flowers from the genus *Dianthus* are supplied as floral decorations for many different occasions, the most popular kind sold is the perpetual-flowering carnation.

The history of the carnation began many years ago when a small plant, named *Dianthus*, was cultivated. This charming name, derived from the Greek, means 'divine flower'. *Dianthus* is a genus of plants consisting of more than two hundred species, some of which grow on sunny slopes at varying heights in Europe and Asia. Perhaps one of the best known species is *D. gratianopolitanus*, commonly known as the Cheddar pink, which was first noticed at the Cheddar Gorge in Somerset, England.

A number of dianthus species make beautiful plants but their appearance was not of prime importance to the ancient Greeks and Romans who grew them mainly for their food or medicinal value. Dianthus were widely grown as herbs. One species, known in those days as 'Sops in Wine', was used to flavour the home-made brews of the time. Two others, *D. caryophyllus* and *D. plumarius*, which had a strong clove perfume, were grown to help disguise the smells of poor sanitation and personal hygiene. These species were the forerunners of the whole range of plants we now know as carnations and pinks.

WHERE DO CARNATIONS COME FROM?

In the early 19th century, Thomas Hogg gave pride of place to carnations in most of the books he wrote. It appears that the old clove carnation was introduced into the British Isles from Holland, but unfortunately the original plants were lost. Also, two very experienced growers, James Douglas and Martin R. Smith, who toured the continent of Europe to find new improved forms of border carnations, brought back 'Germania', the progenitor of the present-day Yellow Ground Fancies and the Picotees.

About 1830 a gardener at the nursery of M. Laceme in Lyons, France, raised the forerunner of the modern perpetual-flowering carnations by crossing a variety named 'Gelle Dr Mabon' with 'Cellet Bisbon'. This work was carried forward by a number of growers in the Lyons area and continued without a break up to the 1890s. One of the earliest American growers, and the author of the first definitive work on carnations, was L. L. Lamborn of Ohio. This excellent book, written in 1892, stimulated the American florists to realize the potential market and led to further development. The variety 'Mrs T. W. Lawson' was first raised in America in 1895 and introduced into England in 1900. This variety created a new standard, though it was not immediately appreciated. When first shown in England it was rejected by the Royal Horticultural Society due to its unkempt flower shape.

THE HYBRIDIZERS

In 1903 Mr H. Burnett, a specialist carnation grower of Guernsey in the Channel Isles, crossed 'Mrs T. W. Lawson', a perpetual-flowering carnation, with an old British variety 'Pride of the Market', which had a similar colouration, to obtain a variety he named 'Mrs H. Burnett' which rapidly became very popular. Another 'Mrs T. W. Lawson' cross with 'Winter Cheer' was produced in 1904 by Mr A. Smith of Enfield, England, and named 'Britannia'. Thus began an era of intense development in the propagation of carnations.

Montague Allwood, when working for Messrs Stuart Lowe & Company, developed several new varieties of perpetual-flowering carnations including 'Lady Allington', a cross between 'Britannia' and 'White Perfection' which itself was a direct descendant of 'Tidal Wave'. In addition 'Baroness M. De Brienen', a cross between 'Mrs T. W. Lawson' and 'Mrs H. Burnett', was also raised and both varieties were successful commercially.

At this time Montague (Monty)

Allwood, who died in 1959, and his brother George were weekly wage earners determined to save as much money as possible to allow them to set up their own carnation nursery. This was achieved by the brothers in 1910 when, joined by a third brother Edward, they founded the famous nursery at Wivelsfield, Sussex, U.K. For a few years before establishing the nursery George had worked in the United States in order to acquire further cultural information. When he returned to Sussex he brought with him stocks of 'Mayday White Wonder' and 'Mrs C. W. Ward' which proved to be outstanding varieties.

Among the better known varieties of perpetual-flowering carnations from Allwoods were 'Mary Allwood' in 1913, 'Wivelsfield White' in 1918 and 'Robert Allwood' in 1931, a scarlet self which obtained an Award of Merit (A. M.) in 1933. After 'Robert Allwood' Allwoods developed another range of varieties of perpetual-flowering carnations, all given the prefix 'Royal' and some of which were excellent for showing. By crossing the border with the perpetual carnation a new range of perpetual border carnations was introduced, but unfortunately this was discontinued in 1941 due to wartime restrictions and emphasis on growing food crops.

The variety of garden plants *Dianthus* × *allwoodii*, which is known as Allwoodii, was named by the scientific committee of the Royal Horticultural Society and Allwoods. This variety was developed over a period of eight years by crossing perpetual-flowering carnations with the hardy old fringed white pink (*D.*

'Shot Salmon'; one of Colin Short's new perpetual carnation flowering varieties.

'Ann Short'. A perpetual flowering carnation. A very good white ground fancy.

plumarius). This gave a seedling named 'Mary' which became the parent of some of the best varieties known as 'Susan', 'Arthur' etc. Other pinks which became available around this time were 'Herbert's Pink' raised by Mr Herbert of Birmingham, England, and 'Pink Mrs Sinkins' raised by the gardener at the Slough workhouse. The muslin weavers of Paisley, Scotland, developed a laced pink known to some as 'Scotch Pink' which is still evident on the show bench.

Amongst the British growers, one of the greatest was the late Carl Engleman, who emigrated from Germany to Great Britain and established a well known carnation nursery at Saffron Walden, Essex. In 1916 he raised two new perpetual-flowering carnations, one named 'Saffron' after its colour, followed by 'Tranquillity' which was white with smooth-edged petals. This latter variety is still grown and shown today.

A further breakthrough in the propagation of perpetual carnations came in 1938 when William Sim, a Scot, who had emigrated to America some years earlier, raised a seedling of superior quality to those previously known. This variety named 'William Sim' was a scarlet and the forerunner of a whole range of colours carrying the suffix 'Sim'. Two varieties, 'Arthur Sim' and 'William Sim' were excellent show blooms and were grown by nurseries for the abundance of flowers the plants produced, which made them commercially viable. However, since the plants grew to 2 m (6 ft) or more tall, they did pose problems in cultivation.

There is some evidence of increasing interest being taken at this time in France and other countries, leading to new improved varieties of perpetual carnations being developed.

However, despite the work of the pioneer growers mentioned above, the trade as a whole could not be congratulated on producing the blooms the market demanded. Up to 1939 the flowers were generally of poor quality, with a very limited colour range and a short cut life. They sold on the London streets for a few pence per dozen and top quality florists stopped recommending them for floral decoration. Carnations, therefore, became devalued as second class flowers. They could only be restored to favour by improving the appearance, colour range and cut life of the species.

CARNATION SOCIETIES

In 1877 the National Carnation and Picotee Society was founded, followed in 1906 by the Winter Flowering Carnation Society, which was founded when a number of interested growers got together. The latter name was chosen as a result of the opposition from border carnation growers, who believed that the society was trespassing on their domain. The society therefore had to demonstrate that there was a significant difference between border carnations and the new winter-flowering carnations which required a little heat to produce flowers in winter. In due course the name was changed to the Perpetual Flowering Carnation Society, largely through the good offices of the Carnation and Picotee Society.

POST-WAR DEVELOPMENTS

Before 1939 there had been some trade shows at the Royal Horticultural Society in London involving such specialist growers as the Allwood brothers, showing borders, perpetuals and pinks, C. Engleman Ltd., showing perpetuals, and Douglas showing border carnations. With the outbreak of the Second World War these shows had to be discontinued.

After the war, in 1945, showing was resumed in the Royal Horticultural Society's Hall at Vincent Square, London, but trade exhibitors were limited by the restrictions on the use of solid fuel for heating greenhouses used for cultivating flowers.

In 1949 the National Carnation and Picotee Society, formed in 1877, was amalgamated with the British Carnation Society, previously the Perpetual Flowering Carnation Society, and became known as the British National Carnation Society, whose membership is worldwide.

National shows of special note around this period were the 'News of the World' show at Olympia in 1949, followed by the 'Evening News' shows, also at Olympia, in 1950 and 1951. These shows were visited by many thousands of people, whose interest resulted in an increase in the membership of the B.N.C.S.

In the early '50s trials of 38 varieties of perpetual carnation were carried out by Mr Hicks of Hordle, Hampshire, England, and also by Mr S. L. Lord, the head gardener of Shenley Hospital, St Albans, Hertfordshire.

From the '60s onwards nearly all the new varieties of border and perpetual carnations have been raised by amateur growers. A wide range of colours has been developed and some blooms are scented, which has proved an added attraction, particularly to show visitors. A number of specialist growers of pinks, following Montague Allwood, have been in evidence in recent years. The late Cecil Wyatt left a splendid list of varieties in the hybrid range to his close friend Mr Whetman, to add to his own seedlings. There are also a number of amateurs developing new varieties of pinks.

CARNATIONS TODAY

We can look back with pride at the progress made over the last century and look forward with confidence that our carnation societies will continue to flourish. The Royal Horticultural Society, in conjunction with the B.N.C.S., holds three shows at its Westminster Hall in June, July and October each year, and there are many prestigious shows in centres up and down the British Isles, besides smaller local shows organized by groups of local enthusiasts. Wisley Gardens, Surrey, England, home of the R.H.S., carry out trials of new varieties and it is considered an honour to have a new variety you have raised included in a trial. Awards are given to varieties successful in these trials and published in the gardening press.

Since you are obviously sufficiently motivated to read this book, I urge you to visit local nurseries and garden centres who will be able to show you which varieties are best suited to your local climate. In the following chapters I deal in detail with pinks, border carnations, annuals and perpetuals, so whether your interest is mainly in cut flowers for the home, show blooms for exhibition, colour in the garden or in raising new varieties, there is something for you. Better still, join your local carnation society, whose members will be delighted to welcome you and share their expertise.

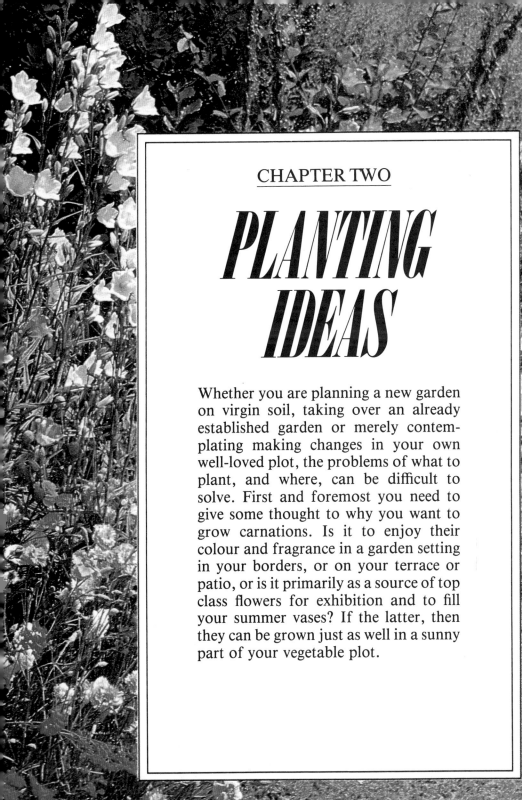

CHAPTER TWO

PLANTING IDEAS

Whether you are planning a new garden on virgin soil, taking over an already established garden or merely contemplating making changes in your own well-loved plot, the problems of what to plant, and where, can be difficult to solve. First and foremost you need to give some thought to why you want to grow carnations. Is it to enjoy their colour and fragrance in a garden setting in your borders, or on your terrace or patio, or is it primarily as a source of top class flowers for exhibition and to fill your summer vases? If the latter, then they can be grown just as well in a sunny part of your vegetable plot.

Carnations have been popular for many years as buttonholes and figure largely in floral art and home decoration, where the many new and exciting colours blend harmoniously with modern decor. This has led to increased sales in florists shops and garden centres. Growing old-fashioned pinks as well as the modern cultivars has expanded greatly in recent years. Planting a few modern pinks in a dull corner of your garden will bring it to life all summer long.

If you are considering planting any of the *Dianthus* genus, it is worth while taking time to understand the differences between the many species of annuals and evergreen perennials which make up the genus, so you can make an educated choice of what to plant and where.

BORDER CARNATIONS

This is one of the oldest types to be found in general cultivation. It was much in evidence in English gardens in the 16th century, many varieties originating in Europe. The plants are perennial, evergreen and hardy, flowering outdoors from late spring to midsummer. The foliage is blue-green, held on a strong bushy plant. The leaves are quite broad and long, while the flowers can be up to 6.25 cm (2.5 in) in diameter. The plants grow 30–45 cm (12–18 in) tall, which necessitates some form of staking. Border carnations need not be disbudded, so they produce a wealth of well-shaped flowers, some of them strongly clove scented. But if you are particularly interested in having larger blooms for cutting, then careful disbudding can be carried out.

PERPETUAL CARNATIONS

This is the double-flowered florist's variety, also referred to as the American or tree carnation. It is a rather tender perennial which can be grown in a cold greenhouse but can be encouraged to flower for almost the full twelve months if a little heat can be supplied. Of course this heat could be supplied free by the sun if your climate is warmer than we enjoy in Great Britain. If grown in a greenhouse, the plants can be transferred to the borders as summer bedding, but they will not stand any frost so must be brought back in before night temperatures drop. Their leaves are rather longer than on border carnations, but a similar blue-green. The minimum height is 1 m (3 ft), and they can grow to 2 m (6 ft), so staking and ringing are essential to provide support. They are usually grown for showing and as cut flowers.

SPRAY CARNATIONS

This kind is mainly grown commercially in greenhouses or polythene tunnels. The cut flowers last for two to three weeks and are widely used in displays and bouquets.

PINKS

Dianthus × allwoodii is a hybrid race of garden pinks. They are hardy and will flourish without a great deal of attention in any sunny position in the garden, provided the drainage is reasonable. The leaves are silvery grey-green, the flowers are less than 2.5 cm (1 in) in diameter and the plants are 15–20 cm (6–8 in) tall. There are many different coloured varieties of pinks, which flower from early spring to late autumn, and some are pleasantly scented. The plants will survive for four or five years without serious deterioration.

Laced pinks have similar foliage to Allwoodii pinks but they tend to straggle and need replacing more frequently. Lacing means that the colour of the eye extends to the petals in fine tracings. They are available in a multitude of colours, as single, semi-double and double flowers.

Old-fashioned pinks are early flowering, but flower only once each year for one month. The flowers are less than 2.5 cm (1 in) in diameter but are carried in profusion and are heavily perfumed. They make low hummocks which are ideal for edging a flower bed or path.

Alpine and rock pinks have grey-green foliage and mainly self coloured flowers. Clumps appear rather like pincushions or toadstools. Annual pinks can be sown directly into the garden soil to fill vacant spaces and the blooms, with stems 20–30 cm (8–12 in) long are very useful as cut flowers. Much of the seed comes from California, and there is plenty of colour choice in both single and double varieties.

Show pinks are grown mainly for exhibition. They have exquisitely formed flowers borne on long branching stems, and are the aristocrats of the pinks. The sweet william (*D. barbatus*) is a short-lived perennial, often grown as a hardy biennial from seed. It bears densely packed flattened heads of single or double flowers during early summer, and has duller, darker foliage than other species.

CARNATIONS AND PINKS AS CUT FLOWERS

For most people the mention of carnations conjures up visions of displays of cut flowers. They are more rarely thought of as growing in beds and borders. In fact carnations are one of the few flowers which are specially grown for cutting, since the blooms look most attractive when viewed from any angle. So many colours are available today that, with a little forethought, you can choose to grow those named varieties which will fit in with your colour scheme, or you can choose at random since almost all the colours blend harmoniously in a mixed display.

Having raised your flowers, it would be a pity not to follow a few simple suggestions before putting them in the position you have chosen. Whenever possible you should cut your flowers in the early morning before they are exposed to full sun. Choose blooms which are not quite fully developed and plunge them immediately into a bucket of water to within 15 cm (6 in) of the flower. Keep the bucket in a cool, well ventilated room — a bedroom would be ideal — until late afternoon, by which time the flowers will be in prime condition for display.

With care a vase of carnations can remain pleasing for up to three weeks, but opinions vary as to how this can be achieved. It is generally agreed that carnations will last longer in a cool room, out of the range of fumes or smoke. While there is no scientific proof to the old wives' tale that an aspirin in the water will help, it certainly will not harm. I find that

Opposite: *'Vera Woodfield' (AM). Deep*
yellow – good show variety.

'Dianne Hewins'. A rich royal purple
perpetual flowering carnation.

to change the water every two or three days, and on each occasion cutting a little off each stem, prevents slime forming on the stems and gives an added bonus of a slightly different arrangement.

Although a bunch of carnations just put into a vase can look like a professional display, you may like to use the wiring method, which devotees of floral art use to create some special artistic effect. The carnation is probably one of the easiest flowers on which to practise this technique since the blooms have a good strong calyx which does not split when the wire is inserted, leaving the form of the flower head as perfect as before.

□ AROUND THE HOUSE

What could be more welcoming than an attractive crystal vase filled with a many-coloured selection of perpetual carnations, to greet your visitors as they come into your home? Most people seem to prefer a mixed arrangement rather than a single colour, but when you grow your own carnations instead of having to buy them at considerable expense from the florist, you can afford to experiment with a truly breathtaking display of a spectacular variety such as cerise 'Joanne', 'Ron's Joanne', a pink fancy, 'Tony Langford', a light lavender fancy, or 'Joanne Taylor', a white ground fancy. You may well be surprised at the reaction of your guests, who could find such a blaze of colour quite an eye-opener.

If you are lucky enough to have a real open fireplace, there will be many occasions when a fire is not needed and you will have to stand something in the hearth to cover up the unsightly grate. What

better than an arrangement of carnations in a vase, standing in a coal scuttle or log basket? For this type of arrangement I would suggest you grow one of the longer stemmed varieties such as 'Telstar', a yellow ground with red stripes, or 'Raggio di Sole', a bright orange. As a precaution against draughts, which tend to shorten the life of cut flowers, you can easily devise some means of temporarily closing off the chimney.

Providing table decorations for dinner parties is often quite a problem in modern homes where limited space precludes the use of large dining tables. Yet here again carnations can be used to great advantage. Pinks above all are excellent for small arrangements, so you should find room to plant in your garden such varieties as pale pink 'Jenny Wyatt' and 'Widecombe Fair', or 'Haytor Rose' and 'Strawberries and Cream', which go well together. Even Christmas festivities in Great Britain can be graced by home-grown carnations if you follow the instructions in Chapter 5. What a thrill to be able to pick your own carnations at this time of year. Just a few blooms arranged with asparagus fern (*Asparagus plumosus*) on a side table with the Christmas cake and mince pies, would make a focal point in the room. It is not unusual today, in many parts of the world, to find a single carnation as a dining table decoration in top-class hotels and restaurants.

Stairs and landings can be rather dark and uninteresting areas in a house, but they too can be made more visually attractive by using your carnations with a little imaginative flair. A copper urn or basket lined with polythene, standing on a table or pedestal, makes a very satisfactory container, provided you have a plentiful supply of Oasis and remember to keep it thoroughly wet. In this sort of situation carnations need to be massed if used alone, but a branch of copper beech in the background and autumn-tinted horse chestnut leaves in the foreground make a nest for apricot or tangerine carnations such as bright orange 'Albisoli', or golden bronze 'Valencia'. Or you can use laurel or variegated holly as a background to spray or perpetual carnations, in colours that blend with your decor. Then again, how about combining three or four stems of pale blue delphiniums with a few pale pink perpetual carnations such as 'Joanne Highlight' or 'Mary Jane Birrel'.

These are only a few suggestions on how you can use carnations in the home. You will have many more ideas but they all necessitate a fair amount of pre-planning before you start to plant, so that you will be able to pick flowers of the right height, size and colour at the time you want to display them.

☐ FOR OTHER OCCASIONS

There can be few people who have not found themselves visiting a friend or relative in hospital, wondering what to take to cheer up the patient. A bunch of carnations or pinks, picked fresh from your garden, is surely the perfect solution. You will, of course, have planted one or two scented varieties of pinks such as 'Mrs Sinkins', white, or 'Paddington', pink, with this in mind. One rather unusual attribute of carnations, particularly welcome in hospitals or even sick rooms at

home, is that they fade rather gracefully, by shrinking almost to bud size without dropping their petals and making an unsightly mess for someone to clean up.

On a happier note, a bridal bouquet of carnations can be just as attractive as one of more exotic blooms, not to mention the buttonholes for the gentlemen.

CARNATIONS AND PINKS IN CONTAINERS

Carnations are not usually thought of as plants to grow in containers on the patio or in the conservatory, but with a little imagination you can create a very pleasing effect.

Both border carnations and pinks can be used in all types of containers but you must choose your flowers carefully as the height and flowering periods vary widely. Your aim should be to have a colourful focus of attention for as long as possible. You will find in the following two chapters a very wide selection of varieties at present available, from which you can choose.

If you are a DIY enthusiast you can give full rein to your imagination and use your skill to make your own containers from wood, plastic, cement, or old sinks, beer barrels, etc. If you have neither time, inclination nor ability, there are plenty of containers in all shapes and sizes at most nurseries and garden centres. Whatever container you use, it is absolutely essential that you make adequate drainage holes in the base before putting in your chosen compost, since carnations will not flourish if their roots are waterlogged. Do not forget to put pieces of broken crock over

'Joe Vernon'. A very good purple variety of a perpetual flowering carnation.

the holes to prevent them getting clogged up. I suggest that you use compost made to the recipe in Chapter 5.

Plants grown in any sort of container are always at the mercy of the owner. Making sure they do not get waterlogged is only the beginning. Because the amount of compost in any container is relatively small, it can dry out with amazing rapidity, so during a dry spell you must be prepared to water every day. Remember also that carnations do need some feeding before the flowers develop, even though they are not such gross feeders as some other plants.

□ WINDOW BOXES

While window boxes are most often seen on blocks of flats and maisonettes, their use is not fully exploited on houses. In these days of open plan estates it is all too easy for passers-by to have a clear view of everything in the home unless the owners have protected their privacy with curtains or blinds, which of course obstruct their view. How much more attractive, for those on both sides of the glass, to see a colourful array of flowers to delight the eye and lift the spirit. A row of border carnations in a window box, preferably of one variety to give symmetry, would provide a talking point when under-planted with bulbs. As the bulbs remain in the window box for many years, you must fix in the canes to support your carnations before the initial planting, so that you do not risk damaging the bulbs. My choice of bulbs would be a mixture of *Anenome blanda*, grape hyacinths, botanical crocus, dwarf tulips and dwarf daffodils, but you must make your own selection.

Travellers on the continent of Europe, particularly on the Riviera, have for many years been delighted by the sight of window boxes filled with unstaked carnations allowed to spill over and hang down like ivy-leaved pelargoniums. Now it is possible to obtain seedlings from at least one major bulb company in Great Britain and probably in other countries, of 'Tirolean Hanging Carnations'. This long-stemmed variety bears a multitude of double, fiery red flowers, which cascade down like a colourful waterfall. The plants grow vigorously, flowering from mid-summer to mid-autumn, and do not suffer badly in a mild frost. If you keep the compost moist, and feed the plants once a fortnight with a specially formulated carnation fertilizer, the only attention they need is to have the old flowers removed when they begin to fade.

Many happy hours can be spent looking through catalogues, planning your purchases to give almost continuous colour throughout the year. Whatever you choose it is important to water regularly and feed.

□ PORTABLE CONTAINERS

It is often overlooked that an ordinary plant pot, whether plastic or clay, can be classed as a container, and the fact that you can move it easily from one room to another is an added bonus. Of course, you can always slip the pot into a more visually attractive container – plenty are available in all garden centres and not a few supermarkets. Here a layer of coarse grit at the bottom of the outer container not only helps to keep the compost moist but also allows you to arrange for the plant pot to come just below eye level. In the absence of an outer container you must at least stand the pot on a saucer. Many a beautiful piece of valuable furniture has been ruined by some well intentioned flower arranger neglecting this elementary precaution and finding out too late that drainage holes actually do allow water to seep through!

Even the smallest room in the house will benefit if you replace the ubiquitous air freshener with a small pot of highly scented pinks such as 'Mandy's Choice'. Some small porches and windowsills are not suitable as permanent sites for carnations, whether growing in pots or cut and put in a vase, since the direct rays of the sun will dry out the compost and dehydrate the plant, or overheat the water in the vase and dramatically shorten the life of the flowers. However, if you are prepared to move the containers daily for the limited period when they would be in full sun, they can play a significant role in home decoration.

One of the most attractive ideas I have experimented with over the years involved using an old, discarded wooden wheelbarrow, still with its original wheel, to act as a container for a dozen or so pot-grown border carnations and pinks. I chose to limit the colours to shades of pink, since there are variations from very pale pink to deep rose. Around the edges I arranged some trailing plants, *Campanula isophylla* (trailing campanula) in blue and white, tradescantia, a striped foliage plant, and coloured aubrieta, which comes in a variety of mauves and pinks, to disguise the rough edges of the wood, and then chose from my greenhouse collection a varied selection of flowers in their pots.

Sometimes I chose a wide variety of colours and at other times contented myself with the many different shades of just a single colour. These pots were nested into a bed of sand and, once in position, I spread a thin layer of small gravel over the whole surface to give the appearance of a planted bed. This wheelbarrow did yeoman service, sometimes at the front of the house, by the front door or just inside the front gate, where it attracted many admiring comments from passers by. At other times it was moved around the terrace, and on special occasions was trundled down to the lawn and put beside the garden pool where it helped to make an ideal country setting for a town-style picnic.

A terrace or patio can appear very bare and uninviting, even when the garden furniture has been put in place. A gaily coloured sun umbrella is no substitute for an abundance of growing plants. In the next two chapters you will find many named varieties of border carnations and pinks which will grow very well in all types of containers. You can always move them around to change your view from the house windows. The urge to rearrange furniture and redecorate, experienced by most people at some time in their lives, is often followed by a suggestion that involves remodelling the patio or terrace. If you have had the foresight to mount your containers on castors, easily purchased in DIY stores, and to plant them not only with carnations but also with other flowers you admire, then you can spend a profitable afternoon redesigning your patio until you are quite satisfied with the result.

A fixed conservatory can be thought of merely as a patio protected from the weather, or treated rather like a cold greenhouse. Either way you can use movable containers to display your chosen pinks or border carnations. If space permits, why not also build a miniature rock garden on each side of your exterior door and plant it up with 'Pike's Pink' or 'Kesteven Chambery' pinks and any other rock plants you particularly like. I have seen this done to such good effect that the transition from house to conservatory to garden was hardly noticeable, giving the impression of lightness and space so sadly lacking in many modern homes.

Perhaps you have an unsightly manhole cover on your property which the law forbids you to cover with soil. You can disguise it though, by placing a large enough container, or more than one, on top of the offending cast iron slab. What you plant in the containers depends entirely on the position you are obliged to camouflage, but for a sunny spot I suggest you plant Allwoodii and hybrid pinks around the edges, and border carnations in the centre.

CARNATIONS AND PINKS IN THE GARDEN

There can be few gardens in most countries of the world which have not at some time been the home of at least one member of the genus *Dianthus*, although in the late 20th century they have in many gardens been displaced by the ever-increasing range of flowers which can be grown from seed or, more recently, purchased as seedlings sent through the post. With modern techniques these seedlings arrive in prime condition and, with little further attention, can be planted out in their flowering positions. This is 'instant gardening', not to be compared with the satisfaction of nurturing your home-grown carnations from seed or cuttings, through to their final glory in the garden.

☐ PINKS

If you are just embarking on the fascinating hobby of growing any members of the genus *Dianthus*, I suggest that you begin with the sweet william (*D. barbatus*). The plants grow 30–60 cm (12–24 in) high and should be planted 25 cm (10 in) apart in groups in the herbaceous border. They are best grown from seeds sown thinly in open ground in early summer and transferred to their flowering position in mid-autumn. Alternatively, you can speed the process by sowing seeds under glass in early spring at 13°C (55°F), pricking them off into a suitable potting compost and growing them on at a temperature of 10°C (50°F). By late spring they will be ready to harden off and plant out in borders, where they will flower the same year. When fully grown the plants bear densely packed heads of single or double flowers from early to mid-summer. The blooms are many coloured, ranging through white to pink and deep red, some known as 'annulatus' or 'Auricula-eyed', coloured in concentric zones.

If you are interested in a greater range of colours than sweet williams offer, and larger flowers, then you should plant 'Sweet Wivelsfield'. This is a cross between sweet william and *D. × allwoodii*, which gives large loose flower heads up to 15 cm (6 in) across. Both varieties will thrive in any sunny position, provided your soil is well drained. If your soil is acid then give it a dressing of lime before planting out. There is no need to stake the plants unless your garden suffers from strong winds, and if you remove the flower stems immediately the blooms have shrivelled the plant will flower again the following year.

Perhaps you already have a rock garden, or would like to construct one. Then consider planting 'Cornish Snow' or 'Pike's Pink'. If you are fortunate enough to find a supplier of the Cheddar pink, which has a longer flowering period than other pinks, then don't miss the opportunity. Its fringed flowers are scented and the grey-green leaves look most attractive against the rocks.

As you gain experience in growing pinks you can look at some of the recommendations in Chapter 4 and follow the instructions in Chapter 6 for propagating your own plants. With careful planning you can have a show of pinks for most of the year. Pinks do not usually need disbudding and can be left to flower freely during the summer. Early autumn is the time to cut back any long stems, leaving bushy plants which will flower again in the spring. Pinks are hardy and need little attention during the winter unless there is a very heavy frost which can lift young plants. If this happens you must firm the soil around their roots but resist the temptation to mulch with manure as this can cause rot.

When travelling in the countryside, you may have been surprised to see small pinks flourishing quite happily on dry stone walls. But it is not as difficult as you might think to establish most of the Allwoodii or rock pinks in an apparently hostile environment. First you must ensure that there is sufficient compost in the pocket where you intend to plant, and that there is adequate drainage to prevent waterlogging in winter. Your chances of success are maximized if you plant very early in spring and pay special attention to watering until the plant is established.

Hanging baskets can be used for pinks. Lined with moss and planted with a compact-growing variety such as 'Haytor Rock' or 'Strawberries and Cream' in the centre and a trailing plant, such as ivy-leaved pelargoniums intermixed with trailing lobelia, around the edge, they will grace any area where the light is good. I find that the best time to plant a hanging basket is late winter to early spring, followed by a short period in a cold frame to let the plants become established before hanging. It is essential to make sure that the plants never become dehydrated, so a thorough soaking every week is sensible.

You should also feed with a special carnation fertilizer about once a fortnight.

One planting idea, often used to advantage years ago by owners of cottage gardens, can be copied successfully today in many modern designs. How often do you need to walk across the grass when it is very wet and should be left alone? Perhaps when you look out at your lawn from the window your eye is drawn to a well worn path leading to the garden pool, greenhouse, or, if you are a serious gardener, to your compost heap. This almost daily pilgrimage is too much for any lawn to withstand, so make a path using crazy paving, or bricks, so you can

One of my earliest memories is of being taken to watch a bowling match by my father when I was much too young to understand why these white clad, grown men should be trying to hit a small white ball with big black ones. But I can still picture the setting and remember the heady scent which wafted towards me. The green itself was immaculate, obviously tended with loving care, but the same attention had been paid to the surrounding border, which was planted entirely with pinks. I later learned to identify the varieties used, which were 'Mrs Sinkins', 'John Ball' and 'Paddington'. This border was the envy of all visiting teams, and attracted much favourable comment from the local residents. I sometimes think that this was the beginning of my lifelong hobby of carnation growing, and hope that something in this book will trigger your interest in a similar way.

'Sheila Short'. A good yellow variety of a perpetual flowering carnation.

walk dry shod whatever the conditions underfoot.

Edge this path on each side with a combination of rock plants including pinks. I suggest that initially you choose a mixture of plants, then wait to see which of these spreads quickly to colonize the gaps between the hard standing. This is the one to encourage and you will soon achieve a true cottage garden effect. Be careful not to plant too close to the edge of the lawn as a mower can do considerable damage. Rock pinks are not only truly hardy, but can withstand an occasional trampling.

This idea can be extended to the edge of the main path running down the edge or

centre of your garden, particularly if you live on an open plan estate where fences, hedges and other natural boundaries are frowned upon. For this choose some of the old-fashioned varieties such as 'Charles Musgrave', 'Sam Barlow', 'Mrs Sinkins' or 'Paddington', which have such a beautiful scent, especially in the early morning or late evening, or after a light shower.

In most gardens there is an area by the shed or a small awkward bit, not large enough for serious consideration. Why not give it a thorough dig in the early spring to bring it to a fine tilth and then scatter a packet of pink seeds over it? You will be astonished at the amount of pleasure it will give you all summer long and often right into autumn. You will not only enjoy the colour and perfume in the garden but will have plenty of flowers to cut for the house. This 'fill-the-space-up' gardening, as I call it, is always well worth the effort.

☐ BORDER AND PERPETUAL CARNATIONS

Border carnations are relatively easy to grow and should have a place in your border, or be used as an edging to a path or terrace. They are very hardy and fully evergreen so their silvery green foliage looks attractive all the year round. Their name suggests that any border will be a suitable planting area, but this is not quite true. Your border must have the benefit of direct sunlight and not be overshadowed by large shrubs or overhung by trees. Unless your drainage is really adequate, you should consider raising the bed since the roots will not tolerate waterlogging. Raising the bed causes a supplementary problem: how to prevent the soil spilling over onto the path, or lawn. You could taper the bed down to the lawn or path or provide a restraining barrier about 30 cm (12 in) high. I favour a low stone wall, which although quite expensive to provide, and labour intensive to build, can be used to support a colourful collection of dwarf dianthus. Varieties of rock pinks such as *D. alpinus*, and *D. caesius* only grow about 15 cm (6 in) high and provided the seed heads are cut off,

they will bloom right through from early summer to early autumn. When considering planting border carnations, bear in mind that they need a winter's rest so will not be too successful in countries where the winters are very mild.

Although an extensive area of border carnations can look very striking, you should consider interplanting them with grey-leaved and foliage plants. Border carnations have most attractive foliage, but it can be rather sparse and their many-coloured bright flowers can be displayed to better advantage against a rather more lush background. Plant your carnations in groups of eight to ten, of one colour or mixed, not in serried ranks but arranged in a circle or triangle. One of the reasons I have chosen grey foliage plants is that they have the same need for direct sunlight as carnations. The plants develop white or silvery hairs as a protection against the drying effect of the sun, which is also the reason for the bloom on the glaucous foliage of the genus *Dianthus*.

Urban gardens are not ideal for grey-leaved plants because of air pollution, and they really prefer open country or coastal areas, but this is not sufficient reason for dismissing them as possible companions for your carnations. There is a wide range of container-grown plants at most good garden centres and nurseries; in fact you will probably be spoilt for choice. My suggestions would include one of the anaphalis family, *A. triplinervis*, which has large grey leaves, and *Helichrysum angustifolium*, which has bright silvery foliage, but you must be guided by what you see when you go to purchase your plants. Any reputable supplier will be able to show you a picture of what your chosen plant will look like and give you a fair indication of its eventual height and spread. Bear in mind that your objective is to show off your carnations, not to swamp them.

Perpetual carnations can look magnificent at the back of the border but they will not survive in Great Britain and other colder climes if you attempt to leave them outdoors the whole year. They have to be pot grown in the greenhouse until late spring, when it is quite safe to plunge the pot completely in the soil at the back of the border. You will need to stake them unless you have already done so in the pot, as they tend to become top heavy when the flowers are fully developed. In late autumn, or certainly before there is any possibility of frost, they must be returned to the shelter of the greenhouse.

If your greenhouse is in full view of the house and you do not wish to fill it with carnations, there are quite a number of other plants which need the same growing conditions. Among these are fuchsias, pelargoniums, chrysanthemums and schizanthus, all of which can be transferred to the borders as 'visitors' or permanently. Using your greenhouse as a nursery for your border plants has the added advantage that you know how tall each flower will grow, so you can arrange to plant the smallest at the front, working gradually upwards to the perpetual carnations at the back. Nothing is more disappointing than to grow a beautiful carnation and then find you have completely hidden it behind some other flower, however attractive that might be.

☐ RAISED BEDS

Many erstwhile gardeners would love to carry on with the hobby they have enjoyed over the years, but can no longer bend so easily, if at all. A raised bed could be one solution for them. Ideally it should be at a comfortable height – about 60 cm (2 ft) high, so that it can be tended even from a wheelchair. It is obviously not necessary to have this depth of soil but a strong retaining wall is essential. The raised bed can be planted in the same way as the garden border, using small, scented pinks at the front, perhaps interplanted with 'Universal' pansies, then a selection of border carnations, and finally a backdrop of delphiniums or gladioli.

A Recipe from the Past

Choose any highly scented carnation petals and cover a handful of them with $\frac{1}{2}$ pt of best white vinegar. Put this in a tightly sealed bottle and stand the bottle in the sun for a few days. Finally strain the liquid to remove the petals and store it. It will retain its flavour for about a year.

CHAPTER THREE

CHOOSING THE BEST: CARNATIONS

With the wide range of colours shown in catalogues it can be quite difficult to select the carnations you want for your particular purpose. How, therefore, can you decide which variety meets your needs? You must also decide whether you wish to grow mainly for showing, colour in the garden or cut flowers. Special nurserymen's catalogues offer specific collections and some include lists of spray varieties as well.

When you are considering ordering border, perpetual or spray carnations it is worth giving some thought to the overall effect your planting will produce and to select the best varieties for your requirements. With such a wide range of available colours and variation in presentation in the catalogues, it can be quite difficult to reach a conclusion, especially when new commercial varieties are introduced.

To help you, the British National Carnation Society has developed a classification system based on colour. Late in 1989 the classification system was amended; where previously the colour was indicated by a letter, such as *A* for white, *B* for pink, now the actual colour is specified by name. Such a system is, of course, essential for an exhibitor, who must know in which class to enter his blooms, and also if he wishes to register a new variety with the Royal Horticultural and British National Carnation Societies.

These societies also award certificates to outstanding varieties, a much sought after honour. The awards, conferred annually, are given in the following classes: Highly Commended (H.C.), Award of Merit (A.M.), and First Class Certificate (F.C.C.), and are followed by the year in which they were granted. It may well be that more modern varieties have also achieved the same standard with or without recognition.

If the symbol (R) appears after a named variety this indicates 'Breeder's Rights', showing that a royalty is due to the original raiser on all subsequent sales of the plant.

STARTING YOUR COLLECTION

If you decide to start growing carnations, one of the first requirements is to obtain suitable seeds or cuttings. Generally, named varieties of perpetual, border and spray carnations can only be obtained by vegetative propagation and will therefore come as cuttings.

Cuttings can be obtained from various sources. The cheapest is, of course, to persuade your friends to give you some of theirs, but this could limit your choice unless you have a wide circle of friends and are very lucky. Another source is the garden centre, though few offer a really good selection. But here you will find, particularly in spring, a limited choice at a not unreasonable price. The best method is to go to a reputable nursery which specializes in carnations. There are a number in Great Britain and throughout the world.

You can obtain carnation seeds from most stockists, though they will not be of a named variety, but they can be useful if you just wish to try some plants in your garden or greenhouse. Having experimented with a random selection, you will be in a better position to decide whether you wish to pursue the absorbing hobby of growing carnations.

If you buy your cuttings from a garden centre or local nursery, inspect them carefully before purchasing to ensure that they are healthy, not pot-bound or leggy, and have good foliage. Also check that there are no insect pests or signs of disease. If you acquire them from a reputable source, particularly a specialist nursery, there should be no real problem and ordering by post is usually quite safe. Nevertheless it pays to check if anything is wrong and, if so, to let the supplier know immediately and confidently expect a replacement.

How do you decide which particular plants you wish to grow? It depends whether you want a few nice flowers for the garden, plants to supply cut flowers for your home, choice blooms for exhibition, or plants to add to your existing border. If you require plants for the garden, you cannot do better than choose border carnations, covered in this chapter, or pinks, covered in the next. Your cut flower requirements can also be met by border carnations and pinks, though for really first class flowers I suggest you concentrate on perpetuals. Then, in Great Britain and areas with a similar climate, you will need a greenhouse with some heat in winter.

If you need a supply of cut flowers you must remember the flowering season of your chosen varieties. Border carnations are only in flower for about two months in early and mid-summer, while perpetuals can be available for about nine months of the year, or even longer. Only in mid-winter will you be unable to pick fresh flowers. Flowering periods for pinks are given in the next chapter. One advantage of carnations over many other cut flowers is that they can last for up to three weeks with very little attention.

The next step is probably to decide if you want flowers of any particular colour. We all have our preferences - some like yellow, others cannot stand it. If you need a particular colour or colour combination, the notes below will help you make your selection. It may be important to you to grow a flower which is scented, and again such varieties are included in the list.

When you achieve your first successful flowering there will inevitably be some plants which particularly appeal to you. Remember to propagate from them vegetatively, following the instructions given in Chapter 6, so that you can continue to enjoy them and perhaps supply your friends.

PERPETUAL CARNATIONS

Perpetual-flowering carnations are only suitable for greenhouse cultivation where heat is advisable, though not essential. The plants are tall, growing to about 1 m (3 ft) but, if left for say three years, some varieties will grow to 2 m. They are not difficult to grow and only require heat during the winter if you wish to have flowers during this period. Details of cultivation are given in Chapter 5.

The actual B.N.C.S. colour code for perpetual carnations is split into two main sections, first the Self Colours, and secondly the Fancies with a background colour. The self colours are flowers of only one colour with no other marking. The B.N.C.S. list is long, with 19 classifications, all suffixed 'Self':

White	Deep Salmon
Cream	Red/Scarlet
Yellow	Crimson
Orange	Rose
Apricot	Light Pink
Light Salmon	Deep Pink

Opposite: *'Crompton Wizard'. A perpetual flowering carnation – new variety raised by Colin Short.*

'Mikhail Gorbachev'. A perpetual flowering carnation – a new variety raised by Colin Stringfellow.

Cerise	Lavender
Maroon	Purple
Mauve	Grey
Lilac	

The Fancies are flowers with a predominant background colour, with flecks or ticks and/or edges of a different colour. A fleck is a brush mark on the petal and a tick is really only a small fleck. The classification is as follows. Each one is suffixed 'Ground Fancy'

White	Apricot
Cream	Red or Scarlet
Yellow	Any Pink
Orange	Lilac

There are two additional classifications: Picotee and Any Other Colour. Picotee is a plain colour with the petal edge finely delineated in a different colour. Any Other Colour does not require a definition; this classification applies to Great Britain but in other countries there are similar systems with only small variations.

Here, in alphabetical order, is a short list of present varieties of perpetual-flowering carnations, all of which are of the hybrid type and available.

'Apricot Sue'
Classified: Apricot ground fancy.
This is an older variety raised by Bradshaw in 1972. The blooms are coloured apricot, flecked with pink. 1 m (3.25 ft) high with flower diameter approximately 6.3 – 7.6 cm (2.5 – 3 in). A good choice for a new grower wishing to enter the field of perpetual carnation cultivation.

'Astor' (R)
Classified: Scarlet self.
Bright scarlet. This variety was not raised in Great Britain. A plant of medium height. Excellent for cut flowers.

'Audrey Robinson'
Classified: White ground fancy.
Raised by Woodfield Brothers in 1987. The blooms are white, heavily edged with purple. The foliage is thin but makes an attractive plant. This variety has had considerable success on the show bench.

'Beryl Giles'
Classified: Light salmon self.
The blooms are a pinkish colour with smooth-edged petals. Although not tall, less than 80 cm (3 ft), the flowers are large, up to 10 cm (4 in) in diameter. Careful disbudding is necessary to avoid splitting the calyx which would distort the flower. Recommended for showing.

'Borello'
Classified: Yellow self.
This variety not raised in Great Britain is a fine shade of yellow with a very short bud not prone to splitting.
Good for showing.

'Canup's Pride'
Classified: Cerise self.
This Canadian-raised variety (pre 1974) with a very wide leaf, has a beautiful cerise flower of good size. It is a good variety to grow and still appears on the show bench.

'Chanel' (R)
Classified: Fancy. Any other colour.
Purple pink base with purple edges, and striped. This variety, not raised in

Britain, is of medium height. Not to be confused with another 'Chanel' raised by T.Niel, which is pink in colour.

'Clara'
Classified: Yellow ground fancy.
This variety, raised by the English amateur C. Short in 1978, has a yellow flower edged with scarlet and is scented. It is seen at most shows throughout the British Isles, where it often wins prizes.

'Clara's Flame'
Classified: Apricot ground fancy.
Raised by C. Short. Apricot bloom, flecked with red. Not a tall growing plant, but very good flowers.

'Clara's Lass'
Classified: White ground fancy.
Another C. Short variety (1982). This one has a white bloom, edged and flecked with turkey red; also scented. Found in most amateur gardeners' collections and frequently found displayed on the show bench.

'Clara Lucinda'
Classified: White self.
This variety raised by Wilcox in 1984 has a white bloom but thin foliage.

'Cream Sue'
Classified: Cream self.
Raised by W. Jeggo in 1979. A sport of 'Apricot Sue'. Non-fragrant.

'Crompton Princess' (R)
Classified: White self.
A further C. Short variety introduced in 1984. This is a white self. The (R) after the name indicates Breeder's Rights which was explained on page 34.

'Dianne Hewins'
Classified: Purple self.
Raised by Woodfield Brothers in 1982. The colour of the bloom is purplish red to reddish purple. It has thin foliage but grows well. A.M.

'Doris Allwood'
Classified: Any other colour.
Raised by Allwood Brothers pre 1930. The colour of the bloom is heliotrope ground shaded salmon-cerise and it is beautifully scented. It is not an easy variety to grow but, when successful, you achieve excellent blooms.
A.M. 1936.

'Fragrant Anne'
Classified: White self.
Raised in 1952. The bloom is white with serrated petals and is scented. One-year-old plants grow to 1 m (3.25 ft) with 7.5 cm (3 in) diameter flowers. They form well shaped plants and have won prizes at many shows.

'Jacqueline Anne'
Classified: White ground fancy.
The colour of the bloom is white ground flecked with red. It is one of the best blooms for exhibition, having well formed flowers. P.M. 1973, A.M. 1975, F.C.C. 1978.

'Jess Hewins'
Classified: Crimson self.
Raised by Woodfield Brothers. The bloom, whose colour is cardinal red with a velvety sheen, has almost smooth-edged petals. The foliage is good but rather thin. Nevertheless it makes an attractive plant and can be used successfully for exhibition.

'Joanne'
Classified: Cerise self.
Raised by T. Bradshaw in 1974. The blooms are a deep cerise, self borne on rather short stems, with flowers up to 10 cm (4 in). This variety has produced many sports and is excellent for showing. Recommended as essential in your collection.

'Joanne Highlight'
Classified: Light pink self.
A new variety. Should do very well on the show bench.

'Joanne Taylor'
Classified: White ground fancy.
Raised by C. Stringfellow in 1985. The colour of the bloom is white, slightly tinted with pink, edged and flecked with purplish red. It has a pleasant scent. It is a good show variety but disappointingly reluctant to provide suitable cuttings for propagation.

'Joe Vernon' (R)
Classified: Purple self.
Deep purple. Raised by C. Short. A plant of medium height.

'Lavender Lady'
Classified: Lavender self.
Raised by Allwood Brothers in 1959. The colour of the blooms is unusual, varying from pale lavender to a deeper shade in autumn. It is an old variety but still a very good plant.

'Mary Jane Birrel'
Classified: Light pink self.
Raised by C. Stringfellow in 1983. The blooms are pale pink self, very well formed, and the plants grow well with thin foliage.

'Midas' (R)
Classified: Orange self.
Bright orange. This plant is a strong grower and the vibrant blooms last well as cut flowers.

'Nina' (R)
Classified: Crimson self.
Crimson with smooth-edged petals. A good variety for cut flowers.

'Pierrot'
Classified: Picotee.
This variety was not raised in Britain. The blooms are white ground with slight flecking and purple edges. The classification is subject to some doubt due to the flecking on the petals.

'Pink Calypso'
Classified: Light salmon self.
A light to mid-pink. Tall growing plant which makes a good show flower.

'Queen's Reward'
Classified: Light pink self.
Sugar pink. Very well formed flowers. Medium height plant of neat, compact habit.

'Ron's Joanne'
Classified: Pink ground fancy.
A sport from 'Joanne'. The bloom is a lightly flecked pink and is of good size, up to 10 cm (4 in) in diameter. It is an excellent variety with strong growth.

This variety has a special interest for me as it was raised by Ron Peaty and given to me after his death by his wife. He had not named it. After winning a number of 'Firsts' and 'Best Bloom in Show' awards at London exhibitions, I registered the prize-winner with the R.H.S. for Ron.

'Rosalind Linda'
Classified: Yellow self.
Raised by Woodfield Brothers. The bloom is light yellow with slightly serrated petals. The stems are wiry. This recent variety is a very attractive cross between 'Cream Sue' and 'Vera Woodfield' and is one of the best yellows available.

'Royal Scot'
Classified: Scarlet self.
The bloom is a brilliant scarlet and is a good example of its class. Although an older variety, it is still very much in demand.

'Salmon Fragrant Ann'
Classified: Light salmon self.
This variety grows rather tall and, while not a prolific bloomer, it does produce magnificent flowers.

'Scarlet Joanne'
Classified: Scarlet self.
A scarlet sport of 'Joanne'. An excellent example of this classifiction but not appreciated by some growers. You may like to try it.

'Sheila Short'
Classified: Yellow self.
Raised by C. Short. The blooms are a bright deep yellow on strong stems and the plant has wide leaves.

'Tony Langford' (R)
Classified: Any other colour.
Raised by C. Short in 1986. The blooms are light lavender coloured, with a profusion of petals, edged and flecked with carmine-crimson. A useful addition to this classification, and it is proving a real winner.

'Valencia' (R)
Classified: Yellow self.
Golden yellow. Sport of 'Raggio di Sole' with a very strong colour. Medium height.

'Vera Woodfield'
Classified: Yellow self.
Deep yellow. During the early spring and autumn the colour appears to be much more orange. This variety grows strongly.

In addition to the varieties listed above, I would like to suggest a few more which are mainly grown for cut flowers. They are perpetual-flowering carnations, mostly raised outside Great Britain, and grown in the same way.

'Albisoli':	Bright glowing orange; medium height.
'Arevalo':	Deep purple with a lavender edge; tall.
'Green Mist':	Pastel misty green; tall.
'Indios':	Bright scarlet; tall.
'Manon':	Deep pink; medium height.
'Murcia':	Strong bright golden yellow; medium height.
'Nives':	Large white with smooth-edged petals; medium height.
'Raggio di Sole':	Bright orange; tall.
'Sevilla':	Large bright clear purple; tall.
'Telstar':	Yellow with red stripes; tall.
'Valencia':	Golden bronze; medium height.
'White Calypso':	White with smooth-edged petals; tall.

Recommended **shortlist** taken from the many varieties detailed above. They are the most popular in their individual classes on the show bench in Great Britain.

'Clara'	'Joe Vernon'
'Clara's Flame'	'Lavender Lady'
'Clara's Lass'	'Mary Jane
'Cream Sue'	Birrel'
'Crompton Princess'	'Queen's Reward'
'Fragrant Anne'	'Ron's Joanne'
'Jacqueline Anne'	'Rosalind Linda'
'Jess Hewins'	'Scarlet Joanne'
'Joanne'	'Sheila Short'
'Joanne Taylor'	'Tony Langford'

SPRAY CARNATIONS

Spray carnations are grown commercially for the cut flower market and only a very few amateurs are involved in their cultivation. They first appeared just over a decade ago and grew rapidly in popularity as new coloured strains were developed.

Initially they were discovered in the U.S.A. as a sport or mutation, from the 'Sim' variety of perpetual carnations. Spray carnations are perpetual flowering and are treated culturally as perpetual carnations. The main difference between spray and perpetual carnations is that, whereas perpetual carnations have only one flower per stem, the spray carnation has many side shoots, each shoot with five or six buds. A single stem will therefore fill a vase. Spray carnations must not be confused with the modern pinks which

also have perpetual carnation antecedants.

The variety 'Fortune', a pleasing yellow ground fancy, attracted much public attention when it made its first appearance at the Chelsea Flower Show in England in 1980. The Mediterranean countries Israel, Malta and Crete, together with Holland are the major suppliers to the florist. Holland in particular has introduced a very wide range of colours. They are also sometimes referred to as mini carnations. The list below shows some of those available at present in Great Britain.

'Annelies' (R)	**'Rony'** (R)
Cream self	Scarlet Self
'Odeon' (R)	**'Tibet'** (R)
Orange self	White self
'Ritmo' (R)	
Light pink self	

The following were raised at a Dutch nursery in Aalsmeer.

'Adelfie' (R)	**'Alicetta'** (R)
Yellow self	Yellow edged pink
'Domietta' (R)	**'Bordeaux'** (R)
White with pink edge	Crimson self
'Exquisite' (R)	**'Manin'** (R)
Violet edged with white	Dark pink self

BORDER CARNATIONS

The border carnation is hardy and essentially an outdoor plant. It has a single flowering stem in the first year and, if left, will develop a number of flowering stems in subsequent years from the side shoots. These side shoots are suitable for layering. If left *in situ* for a few years the plants tend to straggle, so it is worth propagating from them to ensure a continuous supply of flowers in a well ordered bed.

The B.N.C.S. colour classification for border carnations is similar to that for perpetual carnations. Those suffixed 'Self' are:

Pink or Rose
White
Crimson or Maroon
Yellow
Scarlet
Apricot
Grey or Lavender
Any other colour

Those suffixed 'Ground Fancy' are:

Yellow
Apricot
White
Any other colour

There is one classification which is 'Clove scented', obviously not a colour, but was included for the purpose of encouraging scented flowers.

The Picotee is a plain-coloured bloom with the petal edges finely outlined in a different colour. The B.N.C.S. also has a colour classification for picotees which is as follows:

White ground
Yellow ground
Any other ground

The following is a list of good garden varieties and all cited are available.

'A. A. Sanders'
Classified: Apricot ground fancy.
Raised by F. W. Goodfellow prior to 1947. The blooms are apricot, splashed and edged with heliotrope, and have an interesting scarlet sheen. A greatly admired flower because of its attractive colouring. H.C. 1960.

'Aldridge Yellow'
Classified: Yellow self.
Raised by F. W. Goodfellow prior to 1951. The blooms are a particularly bright canary yellow. The plants have good foliage. A.M. 1951.

'Alfriston'
Classified: Scarlet self.
Scarlet blooms borne on short stiff stems. It has good foliage and vigorous growth.

'Angelo'
Classified: Yellow ground fancy.
Raised by Douglas in 1964. The blooms are yellow, edged and marked deep purple.

'Belle of Bookham'
Classified: Any other colour self.
Raised by Douglas in 1937. The blooms are old rose self. These plants have one disadvantage in that the stems are long and thin, sometimes not being strong enough to carry the flower without drooping. A.M. 1947.

'Bookham Peach'
Classified: Pink self.
A beautifully clear pink bloom.

'Bookham Perfume'
Classified: Crimson self.
Raised by Douglas in 1939. The blooms are maroon self and clove scented.

'Nichola Ann'. A border carnation: one of the best white selfs for exhibition.

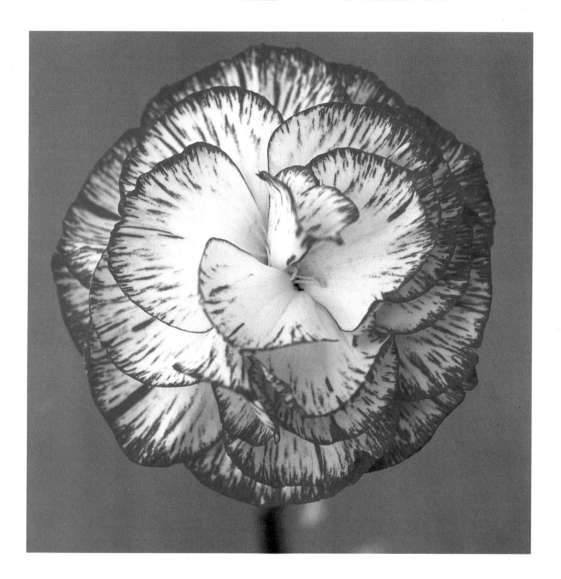

'Bookham Lad'. A border carnation – a good white ground fancy for show purposes.

'Bookham Spice'
Classified: White self.
Unusually bright white sheen to the blooms. Highly scented. Short foliage for a border variety.

'Bookham Sprite'
Classified: White ground fancy.
The blooms are snowy white, heavily edged and striped with a deep cherry red.

'Brian Tumbler'
Classified: Yellow ground fancy.
The blooms are yellow, evenly striped and edged salmon red. This plant grows strongly.

'Bryony Lisa'
Classified: White ground fancy.
The blooms are white, marked and edged in pink. A very good variety to grow.

'Butterfly'
Classified: Any other colour fancy.
Raised by C. H. Herbert in 1932. The blooms are grey ground flaked with carmine. An unusual colour combination.

'Catherine Glover'
Classified: Yellow ground fancy.
Raised by Douglas in 1939. The blooms are yellow barred scarlet. One of the good old exhibition varieties.

'Clarabelle'
Classified: Grey self.
Raised by W. G. Ferris in 1952. The blooms are lavender grey self. F.C.C. 1968.

'Clunie'
Classified: Apricot self.
Raised by Douglas in 1957. The blooms are apricot coloured A.M. 1975.

'Edenside White'
Classified: White self.
A white bloom of excellent form and consistency. A.M.

'Eileen O'Connor'
Classified: Apricot self.
Raised by J. Galbally in 1977. The blooms are a pretty apricot colour and scented.

'Elizabeth Nelson'
Classified: White ground fancy.
Raised by A. Fulton in 1947. The blooms are white with crimson purple to oxblood red markings.

'Eppie'
Classified: Yellow self.
Raised by J. Galbally in 1977. The blooms are bright yellow.

'Eudoxia'
Classified: White self.
Raised by Douglas in 1958. The blooms are white and have proved good for exhibition.

'Eva Humphries'
Classified: White ground picotee.
Raised by J. H. Humphries before 1946. The blooms are white with purple edges. One of the best to grow. F.C.C. 1947.

'Exquisite'
Classified: Pink self.
Raised by Douglas in 1942. The blooms are rose pink, the plant being a sport from 'Afton Water'.

'Fiery Cross'
Classified: Scarlet self.
Raised by Douglas in 1949. The blooms are scarlet and clove scented. F.C.C. 1971.

'Golden Cross'
Classified: Yellow self.
Good shaped yellow bloom. The plant
has a compact, robust habit.

'Grey Dove'
Classified: Grey self.
The blooms are heliotrope-grey, of
consistently good shape borne on
compact plants.

'Hannah Louise'
Classified: Yellow ground picotee.
Raised by J. Galbally in 1974. The
blooms are yellow, edged scarlet. A.M.
1982.

'Harmony'
Classified: Any other colour fancy.
The blooms are coloured French grey,
banded and striped bright scarlet cerise.
This is a very popular plant.

'Jean Knight'
Classified: White ground fancy.
Raised by R. H. Knight in 1974. The
blooms are white striped with purple.

'Jenny Kerridge'
Classified: Yellow ground fancy.
Raised by E. H. Kerridge before 1968.
The blooms are yellow striped with rosy
purple.

'Jolene'
Classified: Yellow self.
A beautiful yellow bloom. Good growing
habit and clean foliage.

'Kathleen Hitchcock'
Classified: Pink self.
Raised by J. Galbally before 1973. The
blooms are rose pink. H.C. 1982.

'Ken Stubbs'
Classified: Yellow ground fancy.
Raised by E. J. Dungey in 1979. The
blooms are a deep yellow, marked out
with red. F.C.C. 1980.

'Lavender Clove'
Classified: Clove scented.
Raised by L. A. Lowe in 1932. The
blooms are lavender coloured and
scented. H.C. 1940.

'Leslie Rennison'
Classified: Clove scented.
Raised by R Thain before 1942. The
blooms are purple or purplish ground,
overlaid with rose and are clove scented.
F.C.C. 1953.

'Lord Nuffield'
Classified: Any other colour fancy.
Raised by S. D. Stroud in 1966. The
blooms are pink flecked and striped
bright red.

'Lustre'
Classified: Apricot self.
The blooms are a golden apricot. A nice
variety with an excellent habit.

'Maisie Neal'
Classified: Any other colour self.
Raised by J. Galbally in 1977. The
blooms are old rose. Recommended in
preference to 'Belle of Bookham', as it
has stronger stems. H.C. 1982.

'Margaret Bingham'
Classified: Any other ground colour
picotee.
Raised by R. H. Knight in 1983. The
blooms are almond pink with fine-lined
maroon edges.

Opposite: *A border carnation 'Orton Lad'. A 1966 yellow ground fancy.*

Another border carnation: 'Peter Wood'. A pink ground fancy.

'Margaret Lennox'
Classified: Yellow ground picotee.
Raised by Douglas in 1910. The blooms are yellow edged in rose crimson. A.M. 1912.

'Mary Robinson'
Classified: White ground picotee.
Raised by A. Fulton in 1969. The blooms are white with purple edges. A.M. 1971.

'Merlin Clove'
Classified: White ground fancy.
Raised by Douglas in 1928 and also known as 'Dagenham Weed'. The blooms are white, edged and flecked in rosy crimson. Strongly clove scented. F.C.C. 1947.

'Nichola Ann'
Classified: White self.
Raised by R. H. Knight in 1976. The blooms are white. This is an excellent white variety to grow, for cut flowers and for exhibition.

'Orton Glory'
Classified: Crimson self.
Raised by N. T. Simister before 1965. The blooms are dark crimson and clove scented.

'Peter Wood'
Classified: Any other colour fancy.
Raised by J. Galbally in 1977. The blooms are pink, flecked and striped bright red. A.M. 1980.

'Robert Smith'
Classified: White ground fancy.
Raised by Loudoun Nurseries before 1957. The blooms are white ticked with scarlet.

'Royal Mail'
Classified: Scarlet self.
Raised by F. W. Goodfellow before 1949. The blooms are pillar-box red. F.C.C. 1961.

'Santa Claus'
Classified: Yellow ground picotee.
Yellow bloom with medium purple edge. F.C.C.

'Scarlet Jubilee'
Classified: Scarlet self.
Raised by E. J. Dungey in 1975. The blooms are scarlet.

'Something Special'
Classified: White ground fancy.
Raised by D. Kellet in 1977. The blooms are white, marked with light purple and are clove scented.

'Susan Craig'
Classified: White ground picotee.
Raised by A. Fulton in 1973. The blooms are white edged with purple. A strong contender in shows for this class and will probably overtake 'Eva Humpries'.

'Susan Humphries'
Classified: White ground picotee.
Raised by J. H. Humphries in 1972. The blooms are white edged with purple. F.C.C. 1975.

'Tosca'
Classified: White ground fancy.
Raised by Douglas in 1954. The blooms are white, edged and ticked with scarlet.

'W. H. Brooks'
Classified: Yellow ground fancy.
The blooms are sulphur yellow, edged and pencilled in orange red. A useful flower for exhibition. A.M.

RECOMMENDED BORDER CARNATIONS

I have selected the following twenty varieties, all of which I would recommend you to try. They will certainly give you excellent results:

'Aldridge Yellow'	'Grey Dove'
'Alfriston'	'Jean Knight'
'A. A. Sanders'	'Leslie Rennison'
'Angelo'	'Maisie Neal'
'Brian Tumbler'	'Margaret Lennox'
'Catherine Glover'	'Merlin Clove'
'Clunie'	'Nichola Ann'
'Elizabeth Nelson'	'Orton Glory'
'Eva Humphries'	'Peter Wood'
'Exquisite'	'Royal Mail'

The above list is but a small selection of the named varieties of border carnations grown today and available for amateur cultivation. If you are interested and would like further information, I suggest you visit some of the summer carnation shows or general flower shows, where you will see many different named varieties. The show secretary will be only too pleased to pass on information about where they can be obtained. Border carnations are mainly grown by amateurs and there are few trade suppliers.

MALMAISON CARNATIONS

Malmaison carnations are grown in the same way as perpetual carnations but differ in that they make bushier plants with much shorter and broader leaves. The flowers are very large and heavily scented but are only in pink or pinkish shades. As the flowers are so large they tend to split the calyx.

The Malmaison carnation is now the least known of the genus *Dianthus*, having been superseded by the perpetual carnation, and it is no longer possible to give a list of those available. There may be only a dozen or so named varieties still in existence in Great Britain.

Since 1990, when this book was first published, Malmaisons have become popular because they are highly scented. Wisley are growing a collection and quite a lot of young plants were available at the 1993 Hampton Court Show.

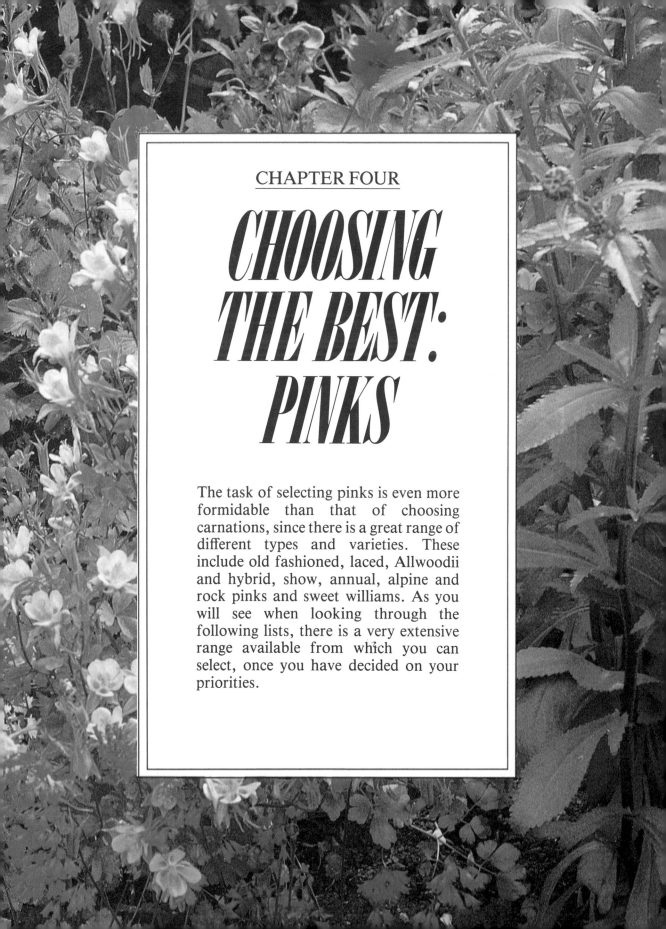

CHAPTER FOUR

CHOOSING THE BEST: PINKS

The task of selecting pinks is even more formidable than that of choosing carnations, since there is a great range of different types and varieties. These include old fashioned, laced, Allwoodii and hybrid, show, annual, alpine and rock pinks and sweet williams. As you will see when looking through the following lists, there is a very extensive range available from which you can select, once you have decided on your priorities.

It is perhaps surprising that people today are interested in the old-fashioned pinks which are still available. Old varieties are still advertised in gardening magazines. Such a variety is 'Mrs Sinkins', raised in the 1840s. They can be obtained from specialist growers, providing competition with modern hybrid varieties.

Some types of pinks are colour classified in a similar manner to perpetual and border carnations, as follows:

Double self white
Double self pink or salmon
Double self crimson
Double self not white, pink, salmon
    or crimson
Double bi-colour, outer colour white
Double bi-colour, outer colour not
    white
Single, not laced
Single with laced markings
Double laced, white ground
Double laced, not white ground
Double fancy

This list was prepared for Great Britain by the B.N.C.S. Other countries have similar lists and some local societies have their own minor variations. This classification system is only applied to laced, Allwoodii and hybrid, show and rock pinks, and not to old-fashioned, annual pinks and sweet williams.

HOW TO CHOOSE YOUR PINKS

The characteristics of the various types of pinks are given below. At first sight the obvious choice would seem to be to grow Allwoodii and hybrid pinks as these plants last longer, flower over a longer period and have very attractive blooms. They are also perhaps the easiest to grow. I would certainly encourage you to grow them but not to the exclusion of the others. As a guide, all the types are of equal merit for colour in the garden, but for cut flowers, old-fashioned, laced, Allwoodii and hybrid, and show pinks are best.

It is unfortunately almost impossible to describe adequately any flower, as beauty is in the eye of the beholder. I can only suggest that you consult your gardening friends on the varieties they grow, study all the catalogues you can find, especially those with coloured illustrations, or better still visit some of the flower shows, national or local, before you make your final choice. Whatever you choose, you will find that all the pinks are visually attractive. Do not forget to propagate vegetatively from any favourite variety.

OLD-FASHIONED PINKS

Old-fashioned pinks are early flowering in late spring and early summer but only for one month each year. The flowers are small, 2.5 cm (1 in) in diameter, but are carried in profusion and have a strong scent. The plants should be replaced after about three years as they become very straggly. This list begins with many very old varieties raised as far back as 1600, though most are from the early to middle 19th century.

'Bridal Veil'
White with a pink and green eye. Double fringed flowers which have a strong perfume. The plants grow vigorously and have good silvery foliage, but an

unfortunate tendency to split the calyx. A very old variety dating back to the 17th century.

'Charles Musgrave'
Nicknamed 'Old Green Eye'.
Pure white single flower with light green centre. Introduced by Charles Musgrave in the early 18th century. A plant of neat and compact habit.

'Cockenzie'
Carmine pink, double, deeply fringed flowers. Delicate yet sturdy foliage. Flowers early in the season. Also known as the 'Montrose Pink' from Montrose House, Scotland. Dating from 1720.

'Earl of Essex'
Rose pink double flower with serrated petals and strongly perfumed. The plant has compact growth and is very good for cut flowers.

'Fair Folly'
Large single blooms, raspberry ground, clearly splashed with white. This variety needs renewing frequently from cuttings as it is very free flowering, which exhausts the plant.

'Gloriosa'
Large rose pink double with darker eye and strongly scented. Flowers early. Late 18th century Scottish pink.

'Mrs Sinkins'
Very full fringed white flowers with strong clove perfume but inclined to split the calyx. Raised by the master of the Slough workhouse and named after his wife. It is said to be a cross between 'White Fimbriata' and a white carnation. This flower is incorporated in the Slough, England, coat of arms. It is probably the most popular of the old-fashioned garden pinks and is particularly noted for its scent.

'Paddington'
A double pale pink flower with a deep purple eye, raised on the site of Paddington Green nursery by Thomas Hogg in 1830. Strongly clove scented with abundant foliage.

'Pink Mrs Sinkins'
A pink sport of 'Mrs Sinkins' with large serrated petals and strongly scented. It is also known as 'Excelsior'.

'Sam Barlow'
Large double white fringed flowers with a deep purple eye. Unfortunate tendency to split the calyx. A plant of compact habit named after a 19th-century horticulturist.

LACED PINKS (OLD AND NEW)

The lacing of this type of pink is really the repetition of the colour of the eye, or a different colour, around the edges of each petal, the petal edges being rounded, not serrated, as in ordinary pinks. Laced pinks tend to be different in their growing habits. After the first year they spread out to occupy more space and quite a number of the varieties, if left for a number of years, get very untidy. 'Becky Robinson' is one of the few of reasonably compact growth but they are generally best replaced after three years. The height of laced pinks varies from 23–35 cm (9–14 in). The length of the flowering period varies, depending where it is

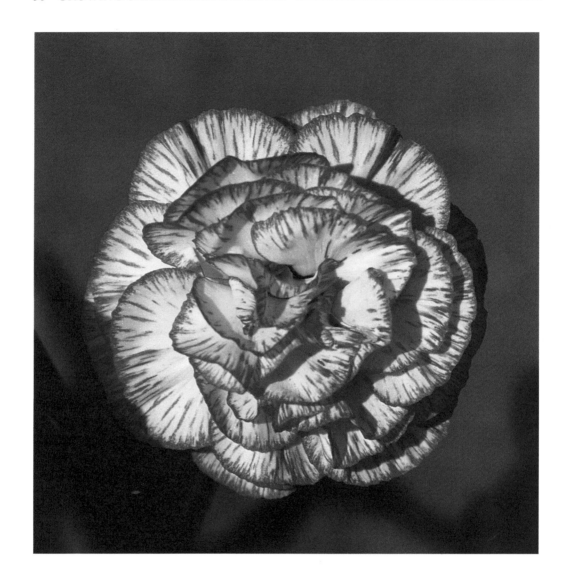

'Ken Stubbs'. A border carnation – a deep yellow ground fancy and a very popular variety.

The border carnation 'Irene Della Torre'. A
white ground fancy raised by J. Galbally.

planted and the variety, longer flowering being obtained if plants are grown in light, airy positions. Generally flowering is from early summer to mid-summer but some varieties will continue to flower until early autumn.

In Great Britain these pinks are more popular in the northern areas such as Scotland, and keen rivalry develops at local shows.

Classification: White ground double.

'Camelford'
White ground laced pink. Clear deep red lacing on well formed flowers. Found in Cornwall.

'Castle Royal Emblem'
Raised by J. Douglas of Windsor, England.
White ground laced red. Large, perfectly round flowers on long stems and with thin foliage.

'Castle Royal Sceptre'
Raised by J. Douglas and an improvement on 'Castle Royal Emblem'. White ground laced red with large flowers.

'Dad's Favourite'
White ground with clean maroon lacing. Fully double with a good shape. Flowers late and long. Also known, as 'A. J. Macself'.

'Gran's Favourite'
Raised by Mrs Underwood.
White ground delicately laced with red. Scented bloom with frilled petals.

'Laced Hero'
Raised by Allwoods.

White ground laced dark red, zoned black. Large double flowers, perfectly shaped. Foliage is dark and somewhat straggly.

'London Poppet'
White ground flushed pink, zoned and laced ruby red. Flowers are semi-double and the plants are of compact habit.

'Paisley's Gem'
Raised by Mr J. Macree of Paisley, Scotland in about 1798.
White ground laced with purple.

Classification: Double laced not white ground.

'Becky Robinson'
Raised by J. Galbally.
Pink, semi-double, red/purple laced. A new variety of vigorous growth and bushy habit. The stout, ridged flower stems are 20 cm (8 in) long, carrying flowers 4 cm (1.6 in) in diameter. It has an unusually strong calyx and the clove scent is powerful. F.C.C. 1988.

'Castle Royal Princess'
Raised by J. Douglas.
Pink ground laced red. Like most of the 'Castle Royal' varieties the foliage is rather thin, but the plant makes a good show flower.

'Francis Isobel'
Pale rose ground, velvet crimson laced. Compact plant with short foliage. Good flowers for exhibition.

'Laced Romeo'
Raised by Allwoods.
Deep rose red, semi-double. Pale pink shading with wire edging.

'Laced Joy'
Raised by Allwoods.
Rose-pink ground crimson laced with crimson eye. Semi-double flowers which are exquisite. One of the best laced pinks.

'Laced Monarch'
Raised by Allwoods.
Double flower with dark pink ground laced and lightly fringed with red/purple. The flowers are 3.8 cm (1.5 in) in diameter and fairly strongly scented. The plant is vigorous and has flowers with narrow petals which have a velvety bloom.

'London Brocade'
Pale pink laced dark red. Semi-double flowers 3.8 cm (1.5 in) in diameter, carried on ridged stem 25 cm (10 in) long. The plant makes vigorous bushy growth, the bloom has broad petals, a strong calyx and is clove scented.
Raised by Mr F. R. McQuown as one of his favourite varieties, all prefixed 'London'.

'London Delight'
Raised pre-1960.
Pale pink ground, maroon laced. The semi-double flowers are clove scented and excellent for cutting. They grow into very tall, attractive plants.

'London Glow'
A velvety crimson with a pink wire edge to the petals. This plant produces only one set of flowers each year, so it should not be stopped. When propagating this variety it pays to ensure that only the best plants are used.

'Prudence'
Pale pink, laced and zoned crimson with double blooms. It is a plant of neat, upright habit and is very free flowering.

'St. Chad'
Raised by J. Gould in 1983.
Persian rose ground, laced with a darker Tyrian rose.

'St. Edith'
Raised by J. Gould in 1984.
Light fuchsia purplish ground, laced with darker fuchsia purple. Semi-double and clove scented.

'St. Osyth'
Raised by J. Gould in 1983.
Rose madder ground, laced with phlox pink.

'Toledo'
Raised by R. Tolley.
Dark pink, crimson-laced semi-double very slightly fringed flowers. The plant is vigorous, of bushy habit, with slender, slightly ridged, flower stems. An excellent variety to grow.

SHOW PINKS

Show pinks are the aristocrats among the Pinks. They have large double flowers carried on tall stems, and come somewhere between Border Carnations and Pinks. Their flowering period is generally longer than that of Border Carnations, early to late summer. I have chosen a selection of show pinks which I consider are the best of the 38 named varieties at present available. They make good plants for pot culture and for planting out in the garden. Generally the height is 23–30 cm, (9–12 in), but this will vary depending upon cultivation. The

'Charles Musgrave'. An old-fashioned pink raised in 1730. White with green eye and scented.

Opposite: *'Mrs Sinkins'. A well-known, old-fashioned pink; a scented variety.*

plants will become straggly after two or three years and will need replacing.

'Show Aristocrat'
Raised by Allwoods.
A delightful pink bloom with buff eye. Very good growth but compact form and fresh looking foliage.

'Show Beauty'
Raised by Allwoods.
Deep Tyrian-rose pink with large bold maroon eye. The large, double flowers are strongly scented. This makes an excellent compact plant.

'Show Bride'
Raised by Allwoods.
Delicate salmon-pink with azalea eye. Excellent habit of growth.

'Show Charming'
Raised by Allwoods.
Pink with coral-red centre. Semi-double variety. A plant of vigorous, bushy growth with flowers 6 cm (2.3 in) in diameter carried on 28 cm (11 in) stems.

'Show Daintiness'
Raised by Allwoods.
Distinctive warm pink colour with faint copper eye. Excellent foliage and habit.

'Show Distinction'
Raised by Allwoods.
Crimson cerise of particular merit. Very good variety with excellent growth.

'Show Enchantress'
Raised by Allwoods.
Rich salmon-pink, fully double flowers. This plant has an extended flowering period and gives excellent blooms for exhibition.

'Show Glory'
Raised by Allwoods.
A vivid orange scarlet. Has a very free-flowering habit. A very striking plant.

'Show Ideal'
Cream pink with salmon-red central zone, and scented. Well formed plant which is very attractive and resistant to calyx splitting. One of the best show pinks.

'Show Paragon'
Raised by Allwoods.
Delicate pale pink. Good compact growth.

'Show Portrait'
Raised by Allwoods.
Perfectly formed crimson flowers. Strong and compact habit of growth.

'Show Satin'
Raised by Allwoods.
A delightful shell-pink colour; scented.

ALLWOODII AND HYBRID PINKS

This group of pinks is also known as modern pinks. The habit and growth of this type of pink varies with the variety and the method of cultivation. When growing in a bed, some present a neat and tidy appearance while others have thinner foliage and tend to straggle. This variation is often the result of hybridization. In general the height of the plants varies from 23–30 cm (9–12 in) but they can exceed this in certain growing conditions. Flowering time is dependent, not only upon planting time, but also their position relative to shade from bushes or trees. Given normal weather, early summer raising followed by autumn planting should result in flowering the following summer. Established plants often continue flowering into early autumn or even later when weather is favourable. Generally the flowering season is from late spring to early autumn. These plants survive well in the garden and do not require replacing as frequently as some other types of pinks. Five years is a reasonable life span.

For amateur growers considering pinks, the Allwoodii and hybrid varieties are recommended as a starting point. (The original Allwoodii varieties are indicated in the following list.) It is suggested that visiting shows and making notes of the varieties together with their colours, will help to identify the blooms you favour. It is worth noting that many of the new colours available have been bred by amateur growers. You should be aware that, if growing from seed, you cannot be certain that the plant will come true to the parent. This adds a degree of interest for those entering upon this lifelong hobby.

Classification: Double self white.

'Allen's Ballerina'

A very good double white. This plant grows strongly and gives excellent show flowers.

'Haytor'

Raised by C. Wyatt.
Pure white and scented. Large double blooms on long, stout stems. Vigorous grower. A.M. 1980.

'Iceberg' (Imperial Pink)

Raised by C. H. Fielder in 1950.
White self. Clove scented. This plant has an excellent bushy habit and is of outstanding quality. Fine for exhibition. F.C.C. 1956.

'Nan Bailey'

Raised by S. Bailey.
Double white flower with slightly fringed broad petals, 4 cm (1.6 in) in diameter, carried on stout rigid stems 20 cm (8 in) long. The plant grows vigorously with a bushy habit and has a slight clove scent. H.C. 1986.

'St. Cuthbert'

Raised by J. Gould in 1985.
White self. Clove scented. This plant is of compact growth with excellently shaped flowers. I strongly recommend this variety.

'St. Hilda'

Raised by J. Gould in 1985.
Pure white and clove scented.

'St. Modwen'

Raised by J. Gould.
Rose madder self. Clove scented.

'Swan Lake' (Imperial Pink)

White. Clove scented. This is probably the best white pink available today. The blooms are perfectly formed and are fully double without any shading of pink on the petals.

Classification: Double self pink.

'Anna Wyatt'

Carmine rose with a trace of a dark ring around the centre. A good choice from the Wyatt collection.

'Diane' (*D. × allwoodii*)
Deep salmon. Early flowering. Flowers nearly as well as 'Doris'.

'Doris Varlow'
Raised by E. W. Varlow and named after his wife.
Pale pink self. A fairly vigorous plant with stout flower stems, 37 cm (15 in) tall, bearing double flowers. Unfortunately it does not fit into any B.N.C.S. classification colour group.

'Jenny Wyatt'
Raised by C. Wyatt in 1985.
Pale shell-pink and slightly scented. A strong but compact plant with double flowers.

'Joy' (*D. × allwoodii*)
Lovely salmon-pink flowers with serrated petals and scented. An excellent garden variety, as it is very free flowering.

'Oakwood Dorothy'
Raised by S. Hall.
New variety. Azalea pink, fully double.

'Oakwood Sunrise'
Raised by S. Hall.
Salmon-pink flowers. Fully double.

'Pink Delight'
Pale pink. This plant is very popular in Scotland for exhibitions.

'Rose Joy' (*D. × allwoodii*)
A rose bengal sport from 'Joy'. Its bright shading makes a pleasing contrast to the darker varieties. It has a vigorous habit and flowers well.

'Widdecombe Fair'
Raised by C. Wyatt in 1979.
Oriental pink (champagne pink). Narrow grey-green leaves. Compact plant. Excellent double bloom with pleasant perfume. Favoured by florists.

Classification: Double self crimson.

'Crimson Ace' (Imperial Pink)
Raised by G. H. Fielder.
Crimson self, double well shaped flowers with 4.5 cm (1.75 in) diameter blooms and a slight clove scent. Vigorous grower with a strong calyx. This is a good variety to grow.

'Dartmoor Forest'
Deep crimson velvet. Semi-double flower 6.5 cm (2.5 in) in diameter. This plant grows well and has particularly strong dark green foliage. A.M. 1982.

'Houndspool Cheryl'
A sport raised by J. Whetman from 'Houndspool Ruby'.
Currant-red self. A good strong-coloured variety to grow.

'Mandy's Choice'
Raised by J. Radcliffe.
Crimson ground with a darker centre and scented. A recommended variety.

'Oakwood Crimson Clove'
Raised by S. Hall.
This is a new scented variety. Crimson self, with flattish lying petals.

'Oakwood Romance'
Raised by S. Hall.
The flower colour is almost magenta. Fully double. A new variety on trial at the R.H.S., Wisley, England, 1989.

Opposite: *'Becky Robinson'. A laced pink, one of the most recently raised varieties.*

'St. Wilfred'
Raised by J. Gould in 1984.
The flower colour lies between strong, purplish red and deep purplish pink. Clove scented.

Classification: Self, not white, pink, salmon or crimson.

'Allen's Huntsman'
Signal red, semi-double with a strong stem and large flowers. Lush foliage.

'Becka Falls'
Signal red, double bloom, but with a tendency to split the calyx. This plant has good compact growth and its unusual colour is eye-catching.

'Bobby' (*D.* × *allwoodii*)
Bright red blooms on short stems. This compact plant has a tendency to split the calyx but does produce some very good flowers.

'Bovey Belle'
Dark magenta. Double blooms on strong stems with a powerful clove scent. This is an extremely vigorous plant.

'Denis' (*D.* × *allwoodii*)
Double bright magenta self. Large flowers produced in profusion in the spring. A.M. 1963.

Classification: Bi-colour white ground.

'Alice'
White ground with red eye and clove scented. The petals have broad serrated edges. A good variety for cut flowers, it was introduced in 1930 and is still widely grown.

'Oakwood Mist'
Raised by S. Hall.

A very recent introduction. Excellent growing plant on which the foliage looks very fresh.

'Oakwood Sparkler'
Raised by S. Hall.
White with splashed effect blood red eye. A recently introduced, fully double-flowered variety.

'St. Oswald'
Raised by J. Gould.
White ground bi-colour, easy to grow.

Classification: Bi-colour not white ground.

'Bridesmaid'
Raised by C. H. Herbert.
Light salmon with scarlet eye. Cuttings of this variety do not root very easily, so it should preferably be propagated by layering. Compact plant with bright foliage.

'Cranmere Pool'
Creamy white ground with magenta centre. A compact plant with bushy growth which bears its flowers on sturdy short stems.

'Danum Lady'
Raised by Mrs E. Hudson.
Mainly red with a reddish purple eye and slightly fringed petals. Flowers are 4 cm (1.5 in) in diameter, carried on flower stems 27 cm (11 in) long. Strong clove scent. The plant is vigorous and of bushy habit. H.C.

'Doris' (*D.* × *allwoodii*)
Salmon with a red eye. This is a real favourite, being the best variety to grow in the open, both for exhibition and cut flowers. Much beloved by florists.

'Grandad'
Raised by S. Bailey.
Bright red purple with an indistinct red-purple eye. The flowers are 4.5 cm (1.75 in) in diameter. Semi-double with broad petals borne on long, fairly stout rigid stems 35 cm (14 in) long. Slightly clove scented. H.C. 1986.

'Monica Wyatt'
Double flower, phlox-pink with ruby-red centre. A seedling from 'Valda Wyatt', more vigorous than its parent.

'Oakwood Shades'
Raised by S. Hall.
Bi-colour, salmon with a pink zone. A short bushy plant with strong stems.

'Oakwood Splendour'
Raised by S. Hall.
Pink with a maroon zone. A new fully double variety on trial at R.H.S., Wisley, England, in 1989.

'St. Wystan'
Raised by J. Gould in 1983.
Light crimson ground with a dark rose-red eye. A good double-flowered variety to grow.

'Valda Wyatt'
Semi-double flower, lavender with a darker centre. Flowers earlier than 'Doris'. Occasionally the dark centre is scarcely visible.

Classification: Double fancy.

'Castle Royal Fantasy'
Raised by J. Douglas.
Rose-pink with darker streaks. Despite thin foliage this flower is good for exhibition.

'Danum Candy'
Raised by Mrs E. Hudson.
Venetian-pink ground, striped and flecked Delft rose and scented. A very good variety to grow.

'Haytor Rock'
Pink with scarlet streaks. A very attractive double bloom. Slow to break.

'Oakwood Bill Ballinger'
Raised by S. Hall.
Pink ground streaked red and scented. This plant is very similar to 'Danum Candy'.

'Oakwood Dainty'
Raised by S. Hall.
Pink ground with maroon eye and lacing. A new variety in 1989.

'Old Mother Hubbard'
Found by Mr Hubbard.
Light rose, carmine rose striped. A sport of 'Doris' and a very popular variety.

'St. Bertram'
Raised by J. Gould.
Purplish pink ground fancy.

'St. Guthlac'
Raised by J. Gould in 1983.
Very pale rose splashed and flecked deep rose. A highly recommended variety. H.C. 1986.

'Strawberries and Cream'
Pale pink with dark pink lines and flecks. A large fully double bloom and very popular.

Classification: Single.

'Brymton Red'
Raspberry-red with dark lacing and eye. A striking plant with blue-grey foliage.

'Daphne' (*D. × allwoodii*)
Shrimp-pink ground with a maroon eye and waved petals.

'Eileen' (*D. × allwoodii*)
Pale blush-pink ground, zoned crimson-maroon. Free flowering.

'Kesteven Kirkstead'
Raised by A. E. Robinson.
Very large white single with a well marked eye. This makes a very good plant with a profusion of flowers. Good for showing.

'Lincolnshire Poacher'
Raised by T. Pepper.
Reddish purple ground with a bold eye of grey purple. The flowers are 3.5 cm (1.4 in) in diameter borne on slender fairly rigid stems 38 cm (15 in) long. The broad petals are very fringed. Strongly clove scented. A vigorous plant of fairly bushy habit. When on trial at the R.H.S. grounds at Wisley, it was still flowering in early autumn. H.C. 1986.

ALPINE AND ROCK PINKS

The original native dianthus, *D. gratianopolitanus*, the Cheddar pink, (formerly *D. caesius*) is now very rare and grows only in inaccessible parts of the Cheddar Gorge. One species, *D. subcaulis* from the Maritime Alps, which is an almost stemless pink, looks rather like a pincushion, or grey-green toadstool topped by small pink flowers. Another species, *D. myrtenervius*, has proved most successful when grown in the raised borders at the R.H.S. trial garden at Wisley. It is about 13–15 cm (5–6 in) high, though dwarf forms can be found. They flower in early to mid-summer and generally require replacing after about three years.

'Bombardier'
The darkest crimson self. Semi-double, smooth-edged petals. Height 12.5 cm (5 in).

'Cornish Snow'
White flowers. Very compact bushy plants. Height 15 cm (6 in).

'Highland Frazer'
A pale background laced and zoned maroon, height 12.5 cm (5 in). A bushy, compact plant.

'Hollycroft Fragrance'
A miniature rock pink. Pale lavender with dark centre. Height 15 cm (6 in).

'Kesteven Chambery'
Raised by A. E. Robinson.
Light pink laced. Compact plant. Height 15 cm (6 in). Produces plentiful seed.

'Kesteven Chamonix'
Raised by A. E. Robinson.
Single laced pink ground with purple lacing and eye.

'Little Jock'
Single pink. Very popular and easy to obtain. Height 15 cm (6 in).

'Mars' (syn. **'Brigadier'**)
Bright crimson magenta. Semi-double flowers. Smooth-edged petals. Height 15 cm (6 in). A.M.

Opposite: *'Constance Finnis'. A fine white ground single laced flower.*

'Pike's Pink'
Pale pink, slight cerise markings at the centre. Fully double fringed flowers. Strong compact grower. Height 7.5 cm (3 in). F.C.C.

'Waithman's Beauty'
Ruby-red flecked with white, double flowers. An excellent hybrid for growing in a trough or on the rockery. It makes a neat, upright plant and bears a profusion of flowers throughout the summer. Height 15 cm (6 in).

ANNUALS

This group of pinks is normally raised from seed which is, unfortunately, in short supply. There is some variation in the number of seasons this plant will survive. Some varieties will continue to flourish for more than one season, some are biennial and some are truly annual. This is in part due to the variety and in part to the prevailing climatic conditions. The plants generally do not have the reserves to survive a winter in Britain, with its frost and damp. In warmer climes they may survive for several seasons. The flowering season depends upon sowing time, so they can be in flower from mid-summer to late autumn. These were once called 'annual carnations', not to be confused with the true hardy border carnations, and were also collectively known as Chabauds, after a French professor of botany. They were also called Marguerite carnations and a few are known by that name today, such as 'Enfant de Nice', a mixed strain of double flowers, and 'Giant of the Nile'.

On the continent of Europe it is now possible to obtain seeds of a mixed trailing carnation which can be used in window boxes and hanging baskets. The flower colours are limited mainly to pink and red.

Dianthus 'Delight'
A very easy variety to grow. Compact plants with a mass of intensely coloured single blooms from June until cut down by frost. They make excellent pot plants. Height 15–23 cm (6–9 in).

Dianthus 'Brilliancy' (Annual)
A hybrid between 'Maiden Pink' and *D. sinensis*. Flowers in three months from a spring sowing. The blooms are brilliant red. Height 15 cm (6 in).

Dianthus 'Fire Carpet' (Half-hardy annual)
The blooms of this F_1 hybrid are an unusual pink colour and open in early June. New blooms tend to obscure those which have passed their best. Height 20 cm (8 in). H.C.

'Baby Doll' (Half-hardy annual)
Perfect compact plants. Large rounded flowers in shades of crimson, scarlet, mauve, pink and white. Height 15 cm (6 in).

'Telstar' (F_1 Hybrid)
Early flowering until cut down by frost. Said to be one of the best dianthus mixtures in various colours. Height 15–20 cm (6–8 in). Not to be confused with the perpetual carnation of the same name.

Dianthus deltoides 'Albus'
Pure white maiden pink. A tufted plant,

Varieties of pinks for the first-time grower	
'Becky Robinson'	'Rose Joy'
'Cranmere Pool'	'Show Beauty'
'Doris'	'Strawberries and
'Haytor'	Cream'
'Jenny Wyatt'	'Valda Wyatt'
'Laced Monarch'	

good for bedding and especially for rockeries. Very good for mixing with other *deltoides* varieties. Height 20 cm (8 in).

Dianthus deltoides 'Erecta'
An erect form of the maiden pink. The blooms are bright red. Height 15 cm (6 in).

Dianthus deltoides 'Flashing Light'
An improved form of the maiden pink. Bright ruby red. Height 15 cm (6 in).

Dianthus 'Rainbow Loveliness'
These rainbow coloured blooms are the most sweetly scented of all the genus *Dianthus*. The delicate feathery-looking flowers are most attractive throughout the summer. Potted specimens in a conservatory or lounge add a delightful perfume. Height 30–36 cm (12–14 in).

SWEET WILLIAMS
(*D. barbatus*)

This member of the genus *Dianthus* is a hardy biennial which bears densely packed flattened heads of flowers in mid-summer. The flowers can be double or single, self coloured or with an eye. They flower from mid-summer onwards for about one month.

Sweet williams have been crossed with *D. × allwoodii* and one of the best known results is 'Sweet Wivelsfield', a fertile strain. A very dwarf sweet william, 'Wee Willie', has mixed colours and starts flowering when only 5 cm (2 in) high and is in full bloom seven to eight weeks after sowing.

CHAPTER FIVE

GENERAL CULTIVATION

Because the genus *Dianthus* encompasses border carnations, pinks, annuals and perpetual-flowering carnations it is not possible to suggest a general cultural regime which will answer all your queries. To get the best results and gain most satisfaction from your efforts, you must come to understand the particular needs of your chosen plants. In the two previous chapters I have given full details of the many varieties at present available. Now you need to know how to embark on the fascinating hobby of growing these beautiful flowers.

It is very difficult, if not impossible, to give precise dates for planting and so on as climatic conditions vary so much throughout the world. The variation in the British Isles between the north of Scotland and the south of England can make several weeks' difference to planting and flowering dates. The planting season is suggested as a guide and you must make allowances for your particular circumstances. Similarly some space is given here to greenhouse management and cultivation, essential for perpetual carnations in a cold climate. In parts of the world where snow and frost are unknown there is no need for a greenhouse as these plants can be grown in the open.

FERTILIZERS

Whatever the condition of your growing medium, it must be borne in mind that the fertility of the soil depends mainly on three constituents, nitrogen, phosphate and potash.

There are two kinds of fertilizers, organic and inorganic, and it is important to understand the difference between them, so that you can make an informed choice.

Plants assimilate nutrients from the water taken up by their roots, so it follows that the nutrients you supply must be water soluble. Inorganic fertilizers are usually easily dissolved in water and so their nutrients quickly become available to the plants. On the other hand they rapidly leach out of the soil, so remember that inorganic fertilizers are likely to be quick acting but short lived. Most organic fertilizers hold their nutrients much longer, releasing them slowly as micro-organisms in the soil get to work, and so they continue to feed the plant over a much longer period. For this reason you will not achieve your objective if you scatter organic fertilizer on the surface of the soil and merely water it in. It must be worked into the top inch or two of the soil where micro-organisms are active, preferably not in cold weather or when the soil is compacted or dry. Inorganic fertilizers are manufactured and hence totally artificial, while organic varieties are obtained from vegetable or animal matter.

☐ NITROGEN (N)

Nitrogen is vital for sturdy stem growth and healthy foliage. Organic substances which provide nitrogen are hoof and horn meal, coarse bone meal and dried blood, while sulphate of ammonia and nitrate of soda are chemicals which dissolve easily in water and provide nitrogen very quickly after application. If your plants seem stunted with small leaves of poor colour, this indicates that they are in urgent need of nitrogen.

☐ PHOSPHATES (P)

Phosphates encourage a good root system and continuous development of the plant, speeding up the production of flower buds. Bonemeal is a good slow-release source of phosphate, while superphosphate of lime is the quick-acting inorganic alternative. The outward signs of a shortage of phosphates are very similar to those of nitrogen deficiency – stunted plants with poor root growth.

☐ POTASH (K)

The presence of potash is essential if the plants are to get the maximum benefit from nitrogen for strong stem and leaf growth. It not only avoids soft, sappy growth but also enhances the colour of the blooms and increases their resistance to disease. If your plants look limp, have signs of scorching at the leaf edges and/or are poorly coloured, with not many flowers, then shortage of potash is your problem. Wood ash is a good organic source of potash while sulphate of potash is a concentrated, quick-acting inorganic alternative.

It is possible to obtain compound fertilizers which contain N.P.K., the most readily available being Growmore, which has a composition of N.P.K. in the ratio of 7:7:7. However, a slightly higher potash ratio would be preferable and this information will always be stated on the packet or container. I recommend a ratio of 7:7:10. Some companies do supply fertilizers specially formulated for carnations and pinks.

☐ TRACE ELEMENTS

For healthy growth all plants must be grown in soil which contains a range of trace elements. These are magnesium, manganese, iron, molybdenum, sulphur, boron, zinc and copper. The amounts required by the plants are minute and lack of trace elements is not usually a problem as most soils contain sufficient. It is not easy to check for particular trace elements before your first planting, but any deficiency will quickly become apparent as the plants develop. The usual sign of a shortage of trace elements is a paling or yellowing between the veins of the leaves.

One of the most common problems is a shortage of magnesium, which can easily be remedied by using a spray containing magnesium as soon as the condition is noticed. A suitable spray can be made up quite cheaply by dissolving one teaspoon of Epsom salts in a couple of pints of water. It may be necessary to spray at weekly intervals until the plant regains its normal healthy appearance. Generally the best way to combat trace element deficiency is to use a compound fertilizer which contains them. Be careful not to use too much fertilizer as over use does more harm than good.

THE GREENHOUSE

The size of greenhouse you choose will depend on your available space and what you can afford, or you could use a cheaper polythene tunnel. If you already have a greenhouse you may be able to incorporate some of the following suggestions, which are ideal for growing perpetual and spray carnations.

A popular size of greenhouse is about 2.4 m × 1.8 m (8 ft × 6 ft), although ideally a larger one, say 3.6 m × 2.4 m (12 ft × 8 ft) is desirable for a serious grower.

In the smaller greenhouse, a single path down the centre and a gravel bed on either side is the best arrangement, but in the larger greenhouse a gravel bed down the centre, together with the two side beds, gives optimum use of the space. The paths should be either concrete or slabs for ease of cleaning.

The ideal positioning for a greenhouse is with its long axis running east–west,

'Toledo'. This is a very unusual laced pink.   Opposite: *'London Delight'. A laced pink; a semi-double, clove-scented variety.*

since you require the maximum light in winter. This cannot always be achieved and, while desirable, it is not essential. It should never be overhung by trees, so that it gets the maximum benefit of all available light.

Since carnations require ample light and ventilation, I recommend a greenhouse glazed down to ground level, with sufficient windows on each side and in the roof to provide adequate ventilation. It would be desirable to have at least two windows on each side of a large greenhouse, offset to prevent through draughts, and two windows in each side of the roof, again offset. This may seem rather excessive but allows for selective opening when the weather is windy. A door at each end can be an extra advantage, especially in hot weather.

The choice between a wood or metal framed greenhouse is often a matter of personal preference. A metal frame needs minimum maintenance while a wooden one has to be treated with preservative every year. A wooden greenhouse tends to conserve the heat rather better and often has a more pleasing appearance. I use both types, but my main greenhouse is a wooden one.

The gravel side beds should be wide enough to stand large pots – 18 cm (7 in) and above – on them but you will need staging fixed about 75 cm (30 in) above the ground to accommodate the younger plants and give you a working area. This staging must be designed so you can remove sections to allow for the growth of plants in the pots on the gravel below. A narrow shelf, fixed a little below the eaves, can be used for trays of seedlings or cuttings. With this three-tier arrangement you can keep all your plants, at every stage of their development, in the one greenhouse.

To minimize the work and time needed to carry water from the house to the greenhouse, it is worth having water laid on. If it can be arranged, rain water from the greenhouse roof should be collected in a suitable container, as it is usually better for the plants than tap water. Even if you have water laid on you should keep a full watering can in the greenhouse so the water can reach the temperature of the compost before use. You will find that a small extra watering can with a long spout helps when tending to the smaller plants. It is not only lighter and easier to handle but also helps to avoid spilling water on to the foliage of any plants below.

If you wish to grow perpetual and spray carnations in your greenhouse and need to maintain a minimum temperature of 5°C (41°F) artificially during the winter, then it is a decided advantage to have electricity laid on. Many good electric heaters are available, the best type to buy being one with an integral fan so that the air in the greenhouse is kept moving, though tubular heaters are satisfactory. A thermostat is advisable as it helps to keep an even temperature and reduces the running costs. Paraffin/kerosene heaters are practical if you keep the wick in good condition, as are bottled gas heaters.

Three items which you will find particularly useful in the greenhouse are automatic window openers, which operate by air temperature to control the ventilation in your absence; a maximum/minimum thermometer hung in the centre of the greenhouse, though not in direct sunlight; and a small cheap hand sprayer for controlling greenfly and other pests. It pays to keep the greenhouse glass clean, inside and out. A wash with soapy water followed by a good rinse will let in maximum light for some months. In snowy weather be sure to remove the snow from the roof, as it cuts down the light.

OUTDOOR CULTIVATION

All members of the genus *Dianthus* can be grown outdoors where the climatic conditions are suitable. However, in cold climates as in Great Britain, perpetuals and sprays must be sheltered in a greenhouse, while borders and pinks can be successfully grown in the garden.

☐ GROUND PREPARATION

If you intend growing any of the genus *Dianthus* outdoors it is essential that you first prepare the ground the previous autumn, taking note of the following special requirements. The area must be thoroughly dug, eliminating as far as possible all perennial weeds before incorporating composted farmyard or mushroom manure. Do note that both these types of compost provide humus but very little plant food. One bucketful per square metre is advisable. Three or four weeks before planting, sprinkle garden lime liberally over the whole area if necessary to achieve a pH of 6.5. Kits or meters to measure the pH are available in most garden centres and are recommended. If your soil is already limy, be sure to check the pH before adding further lime.

☐ SITING

The site chosen should be light and airy and free from overhanging trees and large shrubs. Ideally a south-facing position will give best results, but this is not always feasible, so you should choose a site which gets as much sun as possible within your limitations.

☐ DRAINAGE

Good drainage is a prerequisite when planting any of the genus *Dianthus* since they will not thrive if their roots are permanently wet. If your site is too wet this can often be rectified by adding, under the top soil, preferably a layer of old mortar rubble, although broken bricks or large gravel can be used instead. It is difficult to give a precise depth for this drainage layer but 15 cm (6 in) will generally suffice.

☐ PLANTING

If the bed is a new one, the soil should be in good heart in early spring, at which point one can consider planting. Named varieties of border carnations and a wide range of pinks will be available as pot-grown plants at this time.

A range of border carnations, old-fashioned, laced and rock pinks, annuals and sweet williams can be purchased as seed. When buying seeds you will find that they are most frequently sold in packets labelled 'mixed', a few are named varieties, particularly annuals.

The seeds can be sown in early spring, either in a seed bed, or in their flowering positions, thinning out the seedlings when sufficiently large to handle. Plant the seeds 3-6 mm ($\frac{1}{8}$–$\frac{1}{4}$ in) deep in fine soil, cover

Opposite: *'St. Guthlac'. A hybrid pink; a West Midlands raised fancy variety.*

'Monica Wyatt'. A very good bi-colour hybrid pink.

lightly with sieved soil and keep moist until germination has taken place. More detailed information on raising plants from seed is given in Chapter 6.

My personal preference is for sowing all types of seed in seed trays as I find this gives me more reliable results.

When planting pot-grown plants in established beds, autumn planting is recommended as this results in bushier plants carried on a more extensive root run. If planting in spring, it is wise to wait until all possibility of frost or excessive rainfall has passed. In autumn the opposite applies. The plants should be well established before the winter sets in. Note that, when planting out in the bed, a plant should be no deeper than it was in its pot and it should be well firmed in straight away. The recommended distance between plants is 30 cm (1 ft) in all directions.

□ FEEDING

If you have followed my suggestions for preparing the ground before planting in spring, there should be no need for further attention for the next two months, apart from regular hoeing between the border carnations and pinks to eliminate the inevitable weeds and to aerate the ground. When the flowering stems begin to elongate, start feeding. Carnations are not gross feeders, so I suggest halving the recommended strength of the proprietary feeds until the bed begins to show some colour, when all feeding should cease. Instead of using a proprietary feed you can make your own. Put a sack of horse manure or weathered soot in a large container of water and agitate it from

time to time, then use the liquid when it has the colour of weak tea.

Weathered soot is that which has been stored under cover for at least three months before being watered down. It contains only about 7% nitrogen but is rich in sulphur and also provides trace elements. If it is used regularly, you will soon notice the colour of your blooms has been greatly enhanced. Soot can now be quite difficult to obtain in clean air areas and where central heating has replaced open fires, but if you can find some you will be amply rewarded.

You should mulch around the plants throughout the growing season, taking care not to allow the mulch to come into contact with the stems, as it can then set up fungal infections and other problems. The mulch can be of peat, spent mushroom compost or compost you have made yourself by collecting vegetable waste. You can even use grass cuttings after you have mown the lawn, provided they do not contain perennial weed seeds or the lawn has not recently been treated with weedkiller. The mulch will be pulled down into the soil by worms, so increasing its humus content, and helps to suppress weeds. Shredded bark and coconut fibre are now available commercially and are good weed suppressors.

□ STOPPING

Stopping is the term given to removing the plant's main stem at a node to encourage the development of further shoots. If the plant is not stopped, it is likely to produce only one flowering stem. However, if you stop some kinds of dianthus they will produce no new shoots, so you must not stop old-fashioned pinks, border carnations, rock pinks or annuals. Kinds which need stopping are Allwoodii and hybrid pinks, show pinks, perpetual carnations, spray carnations and laced pinks.

□ DISBUDDING

To secure larger flowers on border carnations, it is advisable to remove up to three buds directly below the main bloom with your finger and thumb. (Figs. 1 and 2) This is known as disbudding.

□ DEADHEADING

For continuous flowering it is essential to deadhead the plants. There are two methods. Remove the old flower head from border carnations, annuals and all pinks, except the modern varieties, leaving the side buds directly below it to develop. Remove the whole of the old flower and stem from modern pinks to allow new flowering stems to form.

□ PROTECTION

If you are attempting to produce border carnations of show quality, some form of protection from the elements must be provided. The cones used by rose growers are suitable for carnations, or you might like to consider making your own by fixing a 10 cm (4 in) square of thin wood or

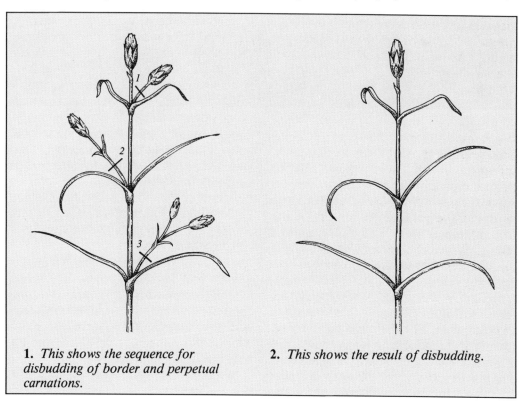

1. *This shows the sequence for disbudding of border and perpetual carnations.*

2. *This shows the result of disbudding.*

perspex to the top of a supporting cane. This protection can be left in place permanently. If you have a large area to protect you could consider a canopy supported on canes at each end. Take care to angle the canopy to prevent water accumulating. Border carnations and hybrid pinks can be grown in pots which can easily be moved into a greenhouse for early flowering or to protect the blooms in inclement weather. 15 cm (6 in) pots are ideal for this. For details of cultivation in a greenhouse see the next section on perpetual carnations.

During the winter or after severe frost, you must check to see whether the plants have been loosened or lifted. If so, the plants must be firmed in again immediately. Leaf litter from nearby trees and bushes can introduce fungus diseases and should be removed.

GREENHOUSE CULTIVATION

All kinds of dianthus can be grown in a greenhouse. In colder climates this protection is essential for perpetual and spray carnations. Border carnations will grow with advantage in a cold greenhouse, but while pinks can be grown inside, there is little advantage in doing so.

Perpetual and spray carnation cultivation has increased in popularity in recent

Opposite: *'Castle Royal Emperor'. A beautiful white ground laced pink.*
Above: *'Cheryl'. A hybrid pink – a currant red sport from the variety 'Ruby'.*

years, largely since people have realized that only moderate heat is needed to get flowers for about nine months.

It is not advisable to plant straight into the greenhouse beds unless they have been specially prepared as detailed below. Problems arise from the spread of virus diseases in the soil which may not become apparent until too late.

If you wish to grow your plants in a bed in the greenhouse, first remove all the soil to a depth of 15–23 cm (6–9 in). Then line the whole area with strong polythene, pierced in a few places to allow surplus water to drain away. Next refill with new compost to bring the bed back to its original level. You are now ready to plant. Even with these precautions, however, the introduction of a single plant carrying a virus could quickly result in the whole bed becoming infected.

In view of this I strongly recommend amateur growers to confine cultivation to pot grown plants, since this ensures complete control over feeding, watering and spraying. If a plant shows the first signs of disease it can then be removed from the greenhouse to prevent any spread of the infection.

□ CHOICE OF POT

Older gardeners tend to prefer using clay pots, which were the only ones available in their early days. But with the introduction of plastic pots we now have a choice. This choice is often an individual preference, sometimes taken purely on the grounds of cost or ease of handling. But I believe the advantages of using clay pots rather than plastic far outweigh the disadvantages.

In the first place a clay pot, being porous, absorbs water, which helps to keep the soil and roots cool as it evaporates in hot weather.

Secondly a clay pot usually has a single drainage hole in the centre of the base, so it is simpler to provide adequate drainage with broken crocks over the hole. You could put broken crocks into a plastic pot, but this is often omitted in the mistaken assumption that the many extra holes will provide adequate drainage.

One disadvantage of a clay pot is the sheer weight of an 18 cm (7 in) pot filled with compost, when you need to move it. Clay pots are also more difficult to clean and sterilize but, with careful handling, can last for many years. Clay pots should be thoroughly soaked in water before use until saturated, otherwise they will absorb water from the potting compost and deprive the plant of vital moisture.

Whichever type of pot you use, thorough cleaning is important. First wash the pot in soapy water to remove any surplus soil, then use a wire brush or wire wool to dislodge any stubborn sediments left on the pot, particularly at the soil level. Then disinfect them with a weak solution of Jeyes fluid.

□ DRAINAGE

To ensure good drainage the hole or holes in the bottom of the pot should be covered with broken crocks or suitable stones to prevent the soil clogging up the holes. If the drainage is inadequate the soil will become sour and often moss will grow on the surface. Worms entering through the drainage holes can cause problems. Avoid this by putting fine zinc mesh over the drain holes underneath the crocks. Small discs of various sizes can be obtained for this purpose.

□ POTTING MEDIUM

It used to be possible to obtain good quality loam to make your own compost but, unfortunately, this is no longer so. It is also difficult to find a reliable supplier of freshly made soil-based compost. Many growers have therefore changed to soilless compost based on peat.

I have chosen to use an equal parts mix of soil-based and soilless compost and have achieved excellent results with it. You can make your own soilless compost from moist peat, grit and sand, together with some charcoal, lime and a carnation fertilizer. If using a 15 litre bucket, measure out 4 of moist peat, 1 of grit, 1 of sand, 2 handfuls of charcoal, 2 handfuls of lime and 1 handful of carnation fertilizer. Having thoroughly mixed the ingredients I then add an equal quantity of commercial soil-based compost and mix again. Leave the compost to settle for a few days after mixing before use.

After a few seasons you may feel you could obtain better results by varying the formula, reducing the peat content, for example. Make careful notes of the new mix and the results obtained. Owing to the possibility of peat becoming scarce, I have tried coir as an alternative in a number of mixes, with good results.

☐ PLANT TRAINING

It is sometimes recommended that young plants should be stopped after forming eight pairs of leaves but as some carnation varieties do not develop as quickly as others, this cannot be a rigid rule. The aim is to prevent young rooted cuttings from getting too tall. New growth must be encouraged as low as possible on the stem to produce a well formed plant. With some varieties as few as six leaves are enough before stopping. Stopping means snapping out the main stem with your finger and thumb – never use secateurs (Figs. 3, 4, 5). Unless the break is clean you will get a deformed plant. Border carnations should not be stopped. With spray carnations, the single bud at the end of the main stem should be removed.

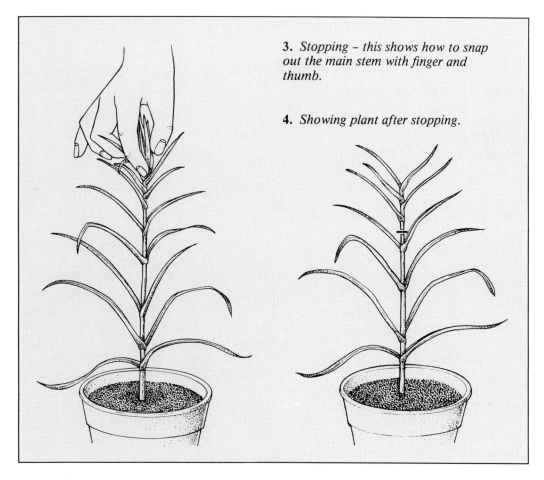

3. *Stopping – this shows how to snap out the main stem with finger and thumb.*

4. *Showing plant after stopping.*

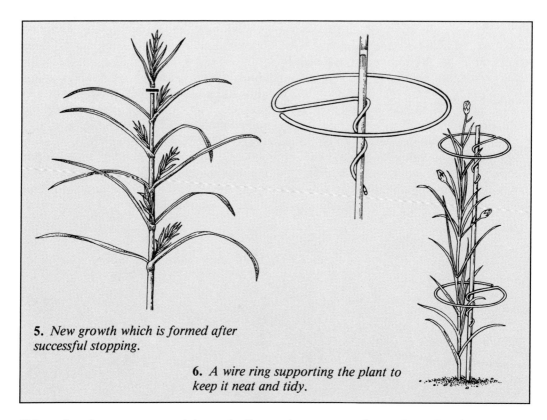

5. *New growth which is formed after successful stopping.*

6. *A wire ring supporting the plant to keep it neat and tidy.*

Otherwise they are stopped in a similar way to perpetual carnations.

After stopping, the plants will grow quickly, developing strong side shoots. They will then need some form of support. This can be provided with short split canes and sweet pea rings.

When they have reached 13 cm (5 in) pots they will each need a 1.2–1.5 m (4–5 ft) bamboo cane with wire ring supports, through which the plant will grow (Fig. 6). Fix these support rings at regular intervals up the cane.

☐ POTTING UP

Potting up is usually undertaken in mid-winter to early spring. Having rooted your cuttings (see next chapter) or bought some from an established grower, you are ready to pot them up in your own compost. The cuttings should be well moistened the previous day and your compost should also be moist. The usual way of checking the moisture content of compost is to take a handful and squeeze it. If the compost does not break up, it is of the ideal consistency for potting. An 8 cm (3 in) pot is suitable for the first potting. The young plants should not need watering again for six or seven days and during this time the roots will penetrate the new compost.

'Becky Robinson'. Pale rose hybrid pink currant red lacing.

□ POTTING ON

The time to pot on into a larger pot is determined solely by the plant's root growth. After four to five weeks you should check the roots by carefully knocking the plant out of its pot. Water it well the day before you intend to do this. If many roots are visible around the outside of the soil ball, repotting is necessary. Failure to do this results in restricted growth and hard stems. The new pot should be 13 cm (5 in) in diameter. Do not forget to put some crocks into the new pot to help drainage. After a while you must check to see whether any roots are protruding through the drainage hole in the base of the pot. If so, the final repotting into an 18 cm (7 in) pot should take place.

□ DISBUDDING

To secure larger flowers on perpetual carnations it is necessary to disbud correctly with your finger and thumb. Remove the bud directly below the topmost flower bud on each stem as soon as it can be handled. If left, it would deform the main flower. Buds appearing lower down the main stems should also be removed successively over the next week to ten days (Fig. 7). If all the buds were removed at once the sudden surge of nutrients to the main bud would cause it to split or deform, leading to great disappointment. Spray carnations should not be disbudded apart from removing the terminal bud.

□ WATERING

Ball watering is advised in the initial stages after repotting and should be maintained

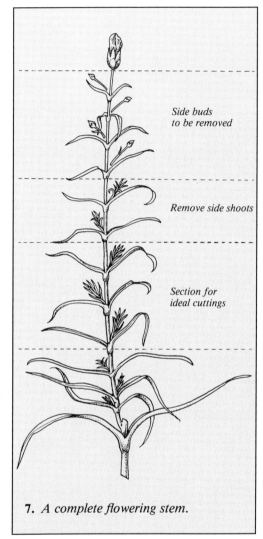

Side buds to be removed

Remove side shoots

Section for ideal cuttings

7. *A complete flowering stem.*

for about a week until the roots have penetrated the new compost. This means applying water only to the original compost and not to the new compost added to the larger pot.

From then on, whenever the surface of the compost appears dry, the pot should be watered. For best results a full watering can should be kept in the greenhouse to equalize the temperature to that of the greenhouse. Particular care must be taken if you are using a peat-based compost or even a 50–50 mix to avoid drying out, since it is extremely difficult to remoisten dry peat. A useful device on the market is a water meter which registers the degree of moisture from dry to wet. An old method of determining if a plant was in need of water was to 'ring' the pot by tapping it with a wooden cotton reel fixed to a cane. Today you could use a small wooden mallet. If the pot 'rang', water was required, but if you got a dull thump, the compost was moist enough. This method does not work on cracked pots or plastic ones.

As the season progresses each plant will need individual attention, as the water requirement differs from plant to plant. As autumn advances and daylight hours get shorter with generally duller weather, the plants' water requirement gradually reduces. By mid-winter established plants are best kept fairly dry.

☐ FEEDING

Carnations are not gross feeders, so if your original compost was correctly formulated, you should not need to feed the plants until flower buds begin to appear. This normally occurs when the plants are in their 13 cm (5 in) pots. A wide choice of fertilizers is available, some specially formulated for carnations. I recommend you to keep well below the suggested strengths. Whatever fertilizer you use it is necessary to allow the plants a rest after four or five weeks. Use clear

water for one week, during which time any sediments which have built up will be washed out. Feeding is not necessary during the winter months.

☐ HEATING AND VENTILATION

Heating and ventilation must be controlled throughout the year. At no time should the air temperature be allowed to drop below 5°C (41°F), but contrary to popular belief it is not necessary to give extra heat when the air temperature is 7°C (45°F) or above. Provide adequate ventilation by opening side windows and roof vents, except when strong winds or other inclement weather necessitates selective opening. During frost it is advisable to keep all ventilators shut at night and only open them slightly during the day to provide a little air circulation.

As spring advances the daytime temperature rises, particularly on sunny days, so increased ventilation is required. This can involve opening all windows and doors to maintain a free circulation of air. Unfortunately this offers an open invitation to domestic animals and birds, so I recommend you to make a framework covered with fine mesh netting which can be easily fitted over the doors when required.

The greenhouse glass will need some form of shading in high summer, since bright sunlight tends to fade the colours of some varieties. Either fit fine green netting on the outside of the glass or apply a proprietary shading product with a brush or spray. This does not wash off in the rain but can easily be removed with a dry duster at the end of the summer when it is no longer required. Before applying to either plastic or polythene check that it is safe to do so.

To increase the humidity in very hot weather, and prevent an excessive rise in temperature, it is a good idea to spray the paths and between the pots with water. Be careful not to splash the foliage and flowers as they could be scorched.

☐ CUTTING THE FLOWERS

Before cutting flowers for home decoration or for showing, the stems should be at least 30 cm (12 in) long. Flowers remaining on the plant should be removed when the colour has faded, with the same length of stem. This helps to keep the plants shorter and more compact.

☐ POT LIFE

When the roots begin to show at the bottom of the 13 cm (5 in) pot through the drainage hole, the plant must be moved to its final pot, 18 cm (7 in) or larger. Take care when carrying out this manoeuvre since the plant will already be staked and ringed and may be difficult to manage.

This is the largest pot size I recommend, since after two years of growth the plants become very tall and woody, and the quality of the flowers deteriorates. But by this time the cuttings you took earlier (see next chapter) will have produced plants to replace them, so you can dispose of the old ones with an easy conscience.

HYDROPONICS

Some carnations have been grown commercially using the hydroponic system but this method does not seem suitable for the amateur gardener.

PESTS

Like most plants carnations are susceptible to attack by a wide range of pests. But today we can control, if not completely eradicate, most of them if caught early. Do not be disheartened by the rather long list of pests which follows. It is most unusual for more than a few to flourish in any one garden or greenhouse, particularly if the grower is warned in advance. It is well worth the effort to check your plants regularly for any sign of pests, particularly on the undersides of leaves and at the base of the flower buds, and then take immediate action.

Any substance used for killing insects is called an insecticide, and a wide variety is available today, classified as systemic or contact. Always follow the manufacturer's instructions when using them. A systemic insecticide, usually applied by spraying the leaves and stems, is absorbed by the plant and transferred by the sap to all living parts. One great advantage is that, if you accidentally miss a small area, you will still kill the insects as they suck the sap. It also persists for a few weeks and continues to protect the plant. Many systemic insecticides are based on dimethoate.

A contact insecticide acts exactly as described. If you hit the insect you will kill it. Many of these are based mainly on malathion, but it is possible to obtain organic insecticides such as pyrethrum. These can be useful if your carnations are in close proximity to food plants and you are concerned about contaminating the food chain. Contact insecticides can be used as sprays, dusts or smokes.

It is worth fumigating a greenhouse at regular intervals, using a smoke cone or a special fumigator. These fumigators are available for the amateur grower and heat the insecticide or fungicide so that it vaporizes. They are electrically powered, with a thermostat to prevent overheating. The vapour spreads as fine particles throughout the house, penetrating all the nooks and crannies. The standard kit will cover a 110 cu m (4,000 cu ft) greenhouse, which is much larger than any amateur's greenhouse. The chemicals supplied will control aphids, scale insects, white fly, thrips, leaf miners, red spider mites, rust, mildew and grey mould.

Your greenhouse must be well sealed when fumigating and I cannot emphasize too strongly the need to obey the manufacturer's instructions to the letter. Do not enter the greenhouse until the fumes have completely dispersed, preferably leaving it shut overnight. Keep all insecticides and fungicides well out of reach of children, preferably in a small locked cabinet.

When you consider using an insecticide in your greenhouse or outdoors you should remember that most insecticides do not discriminate between insects. They kill all they reach, including ladybirds which do no harm but actually thrive on a diet of greenfly. It is best to spray in the evening when the bees are not active. Some insecticides are claimed to be less lethal to certain insects than others – pirimicarb is one. It is claimed that it does not kill ladybirds, lacewings and bees, if used as recommended, but it still kills aphids. Unless the insects are causing real damage it is kinder to live with them.

There are now biological controls for some insect pests, but an amateur grower, even with a large number of plants, might not find these small insectivores really practical.

□ ANTS
Ants themselves do little damage but they carry greenfly from one plant to another. Their runs can often be seen and a commercial ant killer used.

□ BIRDS
Birds can do considerable damage to outdoor carnations and pinks by eating the growing buds. The only effective deterrent is netting or black cotton which may be less noticeable.

□ CARNATION FLY
This pest, sometimes called the leaf miner or carnation maggot, can be a problem on outdoor carnations and pinks. The fly lays its eggs on the upper part of leaf joints and after hatching the maggots tunnel into the leaves and stems. An invasion of this pest is recognizable by the white streaks on the leaves and stems. The danger period is from late spring to mid-summer.

Control this pest by spraying with a systemic insecticide or dust the plants with derris. Alternatively, dust with well weathered soot.

□ CATERPILLARS (*Tortrix moth*)
This yellowish green caterpillar with a brown head is about 2 cm (0.75 in) long. It is active at night, attacking new growth, buds and flowers. The simplest and most effective control is to pick them off by torchlight and destroy them. They can

also be killed by insecticides containing gamma-HCH or derris powder. Smoke cones are also effective, but only if your greenhouse can be well sealed.

□ CUTWORM

This caterpillar which forages on the surface of the soil occasionally attacks outdoor carnations. Control is simplest by picking off at night by torchlight. Alternatively, if these pests are a real problem, work bromophos into the surface soil.

□ EARWIGS

Carnation flowers are particularly attractive to earwigs and can be extensively damaged. These pests are difficult to control with chemicals and so are best dealt with in the old-fashioned way by putting inverted pots, stuffed with hay or dry moss, on top of canes placed at intervals among the plants. The earwigs collect overnight and can be disposed of in the morning.

□ EELWORMS

These almost invisible worms can be present in soil, leaf mould and manure and, if introduced into the greenhouse, can be a positive menace. They lay eggs in the root tissues and can quickly destroy the whole plant. There is no known cure once the plant has been attacked, but sterilizing the potting medium and good greenhouse hygiene will prevent their introduction. It is good practice to remove any infected plant from the greenhouse, burn it, and do not use the soil from the pot again.

□ GREENFLY

This aphid can pose a real problem, as it multiplies at an alarming rate, excreting a sticky liquid which attracts other pests. You will probably also notice a black fungus on the plant which badly disfigures it. Even more important, in my opinion, is the fact that greenfly can transmit virus diseases which will only become apparent later in the form of yellow streaks or spots on the foliage.

The principal danger periods are spring and autumn, so some growers spray every 10 to 14 days at these times, but at longer intervals during the summer. Since commercial insecticides should not normally be stored after mixing, it can be more economical and just as effective to keep a close watch on the undersides of the leaves and growing tips, the favourite feeding places of greenfly. Then spray immediately you spot them.

□ RED SPIDER MITE
(*Tetranychus urticae*)

This sucking mite is, in fact, neither red nor a spider. It is an extemely tiny yellow or brownish mite, less than 0.5 mm (0.02 in) long, which can only be seen with the naked eye when a colony has formed, looking like a type of rust on the undersides of the leaves. The mites and their webs can be seen with a magnifying glass. It is usually noticed first on the lower leaves and spreads rapidly to all parts of the plant. Leaves soon display small white scars and lose their waxy appearance, becoming a dull grey. Eventually the leaf, and finally the whole plant, will die if no effective action is taken. Plants in the near vicinity will almost certainly be infected very rapidly as the red spider mites spread through the whole greenhouse.

Unfortunately they are difficult to eradicate, once you have identified the problem. Two methods are available, one trying to create an atmosphere not conducive to their lifestyle, while the other attempts to kill them off.

As they prefer a dry, hot atmosphere, you can increase the humidity by keeping the paths wet and any spaces between the plants moist. Ventilation must be at maximum and shading is advisable in very sunny weather to reduce the temperature. It is sometimes suggested that the plants themselves should be sprayed with water, but this is better avoided to reduce the risk of fungal diseases. However, where there is severe infestation, take the plant in its pot outside on to a path, lay it on its side and hose off the colonies of mites.

The second method, best practised at the same time as the first, is to attack the mites with insecticide, preferably systemic, spraying the plant and watering the soil in the pot. This will need to be repeated at seven-day intervals.

If, despite your best efforts, the infestation persists, the plant should be burnt. If all the plants in your greenhouse become badly infested then you must sadly consider burning them, cleaning and fumigating the greenhouse, and starting all over again.

□ SLUGS

Primarily an outdoor problem, these pests emerge at night, feeding voraciously on new growth. They can do considerable damage. They can be collected by torchlight and disposed of, or you can use one of the brands of slug pellet. Cover the pellets with small tiles, or something similar, so that the slugs can reach the bait but birds, hedgehogs and domestic animals are not at risk. A slug killer which can be watered in around seedlings is now available and I have found this to be effective. It is not poisonous to birds and domestic pets.

□ THRIPS

These minute winged insects usually attack the flower buds. They feed by sucking sap from the unopened bud, resulting in irregular white patches on the petals when the flowers open – most noticeable on dark-hued blooms. One popular means of control is to dust the lower parts of the plant together with all surfaces below plant level in the greenhouse with gamma-HCH or derris powder. Systemic insecticides are also effective. The danger period is from mid-spring to early summer.

□ WHITEFLY

This is another aphid, but one that seldom causes a problem if carnations are grown in isolation. But if carnations are grown in a greenhouse with aubergines or peppers, there can be a cross infection from these susceptible plants. Treat as for greenfly but as whitefly eggs are not killed by the spray, you will need to repeat the treatment every seven days.

□ WIREWORMS

These mainly affect outdoor carnations and pinks but can get into greenhouse cultivation. They are small yellowish brown, string-like creatures which attack the roots and base of the stem, causing the plant to collapse without obvious cause. They are particularly prevalent on newly cultivated land. An old remedy was to bury small pieces of carrot, marked with sticks so that you can find them, just beneath the surface of the soil. These attracted the pests which could then be removed and destroyed. Otherwise rake in some bromophos.

☐ WOODLICE

Another night predator which eats the leaves and stems, particularly new growth. They hide in debris by day, so are best controlled by paying attention to greenhouse hygiene. Outside they can be a particular problem on pinks growing on a rockery, as they hide under the stones. But they can be trapped by placing pieces of scooped out potato or root vegatable in the vicinity, which can be disposed of periodically.

☐ WORMS

The ordinary garden worm is an asset to the garden, but not in pots in the greenhouse. They can easily be removed by watering the pot with lime water, which causes them to come to the surface where they can be picked off.

DISEASES

Carnations and pinks grown outdoors are much less susceptible to diseases than those cultivated in a greenhouse. Diseases are caused by fungi, bacteria and viruses. A wide range of products is sold for attacking fungal diseases, including systemic and contact fungicides, but those caused by bacteria and viruses are much more difficult to control.

It cannot be over-emphasized that the correct cultural conditions, and attention to hygiene, are essential in the greenhouse if disease is to be avoided. When purchasing new plants, inspect them thoroughly to ensure, as far as possible, that they are free from disease. Otherwise you run the risk of infecting all your healthy plants.

It is always advisable to clean and disinfect the whole greenhouse each year with a product such as Jeyes fluid, preferably in autumn. The glass, staging, pots, walkways, in fact everything in the greenhouse, should be thoroughly cleaned to keep disease to a minimum. You will never achieve complete freedom from disease but will only rarely meet one or two of the following depressingly long list of possibles.

☐ ANTHER SMUT

A soot-like fungus which attacks the plants, particularly the flowers. The pollen sacks on the anthers will go black and, as there is no known cure, the plant should be burnt.

☐ DAMPING OFF

This disease is caused by a fungus which spreads on the surface of the soil, attacking seedlings and newly planted cuttings. A whole tray of seedlings can be destroyed in one night. Prevention being better than cure, use only sterilized

Opposite: *Allwoodii hybrid pink 'Iceberg' – a sport of the well-known 'Doris'.*

potting compost. If in doubt, spray with Cheshunt Compound or benomyl.

☐ FUSARIUM WILT (*Fusarium dianthi*)

Another fatal disease, identified by the withering of a single branch. The leaves first become dull, then turn brown. Do not be tempted to remove this branch as it is already too late to save the plant. Remove the potted plant from the greenhouse, burn the plant, dispose of the soil and disinfect the pot with a solution of Jeyes fluid.

If the problem occurs outdoors, re-move and destroy the plant and dress the ground with lime.

☐ LEAF SPOT (*Alternaria dianthi*)

Rather similar to rust in appearance but leaf spot has a brownish centre with a purplish black ring outside it. It is also caused by warm damp conditions, as found in a wet summer or humid green-house. Remove and burn the infected leaves, taking care not to spread infection to other plants, and treat with benomyl.

☐ MILDEW (*Oidium dianthi*)

This treatable disease is seen as a white powdery fungus on the leaves, stems and buds. If untreated the plants will eventually die. Early treatment is important as the fungus spreads very rapidly. Dusting with green sulphur or spraying with benomyl should cure the problem, though a second application about a week later may be necessary. Mildew thrives in close, airless conditions, so provide adequate ventilation in the greenhouse to minimize the risk.

☐ RUST (*Uromyces dianthi*)

A fungal disease first identified in 1892, when it became so prevalent that some growers abandoned carnations. It is perhaps the most common disease affecting the genus *Dianthus*. It first appears as small brownish marks on both sides of the leaves which split open, releasing bright spores which spread the disease to other plants on the air currents.

As soon as you notice the tell-tale marks, pick off and burn the infected leaves, being careful not to spread the fungus to other plants on your hands. It thrives in warm, humid conditions, so can be discouraged by adequate ventilation. If you are already waging war on red spider mite by raising the humidity, I suggest that you damp down against the mite in the morning to ensure that the leaves are dry before closing up at night. Effective treatments are spraying with Bordeaux mixture or dusting with a fungicide containing mancozeb.

☐ STEM ROT

This fatal disease can normally be avoided, given good cultural conditions. It flourishes where drainage is bad or where planting has been too deep, either in pots or in the garden. It cannot be easily identified, as the plant just wilts and dies, and there is nothing you can do to save it.

☐ VIRUS DISEASES

There are many virus diseases, most of which do not really affect plant growth or appearance. There is no known cure for any of them, but as the disease is mainly spread by greenfly, controlling this pest should prevent the problem arising. The usual symptoms which indicate the presence of a virus are faint mottling or spots on the leaves, and in more serious cases distorted leaves.

DISORDERS

Some problems that arise when cultivating carnations cannot be classed as due to pests or diseases, but are mainly of physiological origin.

Disorders often appear due to unbalanced feeding. A deficiency of potash leads to leaf tip burn, white spotting and partial chlorosis, while boron deficiency produces weak auxiliary shoots below the terminal bud, browning of the leaf tips, bands of red/purple pigments and again partial chlorosis. Good cultivation and feeding prevent these disorders.

☐ CALYX SPLITTING

A well-known problem caused by several factors, either alone or in combination. Sudden extreme fluctuations in temperature, overwatering a dry plant, poor feeding, particularly an imbalance between nitrogen and potash, are all possible causes. Good cultivation will avoid this problem. Unfortunately some varieties of carnations are known to be prone to this problem and little can be done. You could try binding the calyx with a small elastic band or wire ring.

☐ CURLY TIP

This apparently serious looking problem is nothing to worry about. It appears in mid-winter to early spring, and is characterized by the curling of the growing tips of the foliage which often become distorted. With increasing light and warmer temperatures the condition disappears.

CHAPTER SIX

PROPAGATION

Carnations can be propagated quite easily either from seeds or vegetatively, and I will give details of all the methods I have used successfully over many years which can be followed by any enthusiastic beginner. Propagation from seeds results in seedlings similar to the parent, though not necessarily genetically identical, while a vegetatively propagated plant is truly identical. Vegetative propagation means using a shoot from the parent plant, either by layering or by taking cuttings.

For many gardeners propagation is the highlight of their hobby, so I also deal with hybridizing. Many keen amateurs have raised new carnation varieties registered by the R.H.S. and B.N.C.S. in Great Britain, or with their own societies in other countries.

You will already have realized that there are significant differences between the cultivation of perpetual carnations and of border carnations and pinks. These differences continue in the best methods of propagation. Perpetual carnations are normally propagated by vegetative means, principally cuttings, except for occasional air layering. Hybridizing is, of course, achieved by cross pollination and sowing the subsequent seeds. Border carnations are usually propagated by layering, though cuttings can be used. Pinks are normally grown from cuttings but can be grown directly from seeds. Named varieties must be propagated vegetatively as seed-raised plants do not necessarily come true to type.

SEED

☐ OBTAINING SEEDS

Seeds for border carnations, annuals and pinks, particularly of new varieties, can be obtained from most seedsmen. Unfortunately they can be far from fresh and relatively expensive, as they have to be gathered, cleaned, packaged and distributed, which all takes time. The number of seeds in a packet varies widely and can be difficult to ascertain before you buy. Best results are obtained from fresh seed with germination rates as high as 90%. If you have to store seed keep it in an envelope in a dark, dry and cool place. While not strictly necessary, it can be kept in an air-tight jar.

The seed itself is about the size of a grain of sugar and no pre-treatment is required before sowing. It should however be handled carefully as the coating is brittle. The seeds are relatively easy to sow but, if you find it difficult to sow thinly enough, you can premix it with a little silver sand.

☐ SOWING THE SEED

Sowing of border carnations, annuals and pinks is usually done in a tray although pinks can be sown directly into the garden soil, in late spring. If you are sowing seeds in open ground, sow them thinly and cover lightly with sieved soil. Keep the soil moist until germination takes place and thin out when large enough to handle. In this case some protection against damage is advisable, if cats or foxes are a problem in your area, by covering the seed bed with a cloche not required elsewhere at this time of year.

In early spring fill your tray to within 1 cm ($\frac{3}{8}$ in) of the rim with moist compost which can be either soil based or soilless. Tamp down with a flat piece of wood to level off the surface, but not so hard that you compact the potting medium. Next scatter the seeds thinly over the surface, and cover lightly with sieved compost. Finally water with a fine spray, taking care not to flood the tray.

If you have a propagator, put the tray in it and set the thermostat to 13–16°C (55–61°F). Without a propagator, cover the tray with a sheet of glass or polythene and place in a warm position such as a sunny windowsill or greenhouse. It is a good idea to place a sheet of tissue paper, perhaps a paper handkerchief, under the glass to minimize the drying effect of the sun. Inspect daily and water as needed to prevent the compost drying out. Germination will take place in 10–14 days.

It is a good idea when watering to ensure that the temperature of the water is similar to that of the compost. This can easily be done by leaving a full watering can in the greenhouse or kitchen. Cold water straight from the mains can shock the emerging plants and retard their progress. I also advise adding a fungicide such as benomyl or Cheshunt Compound to the water to prevent damping off, as this can be a serious problem in the early stages of growth. When the seedlings are clearly visible, remove the cover from the tray, or they will grow lanky and fail to produce good plants. Maximum light and air are important at this stage.

Seeds of sweet williams (*D. barbatus*) are treated rather differently, as this is a hardy biennial variety. It is usually sown 6 mm ($\frac{1}{4}$ in) deep in mid-summer, either in a seed tray or a well-prepared seed bed. When the seedlings are a reasonable size in mid-autumn, they are transferred to their flowering positions for the next year. In my experience sweet williams attract more than their fair share of slugs, so keep watch and take remedial action. Despite it being a biennial, you can sow the seeds in mid-spring to early summer to get flowers in the same year.

☐ PRICKING OUT

The first two leaves which appear are the cotyledon, quickly followed by two true carnation leaves. At this stage the seedlings are ready for pricking out, which means transferring them to another area where they will have more room to develop. Prepare another seed tray similar to the first but preferably slightly deeper. Take great care when moving the seed-lings, as they are very delicate. Seedlings should never be taken from the seed tray by gripping the roots or stem but gently lifted holding the seed leaf between the finger and thumb. If you first loosen the compost around the seedlings with a spatula, beginning at the side of the tray, the job is simplified and you will do minimum damage.

I recommend setting the transplanted seedlings 5 cm (2 in) apart in all directions, so you get 40 in a normal-sized seed tray. Plant each seedling at the same depth as in the original tray and firm in gently. Pricking out is made much easier if you use a pencil or other small dibber to make a hole in the compost large enough to receive the roots. Firming is necessary to remove any air pockets you may have introduced. If you prefer, you can pass over this stage of pricking out into a seed tray and transplant straight into an 8 cm (3 in) pot. The trays or pots can now be stood in a greenhouse, cold frame or on a windowsill where they will get both light and air.

It is unlikely that these seedlings will need feeding at this stage but you must ensure that the compost does not dry out. They generally require little attention until they are 5 cm (2 in) high, when they are ready to be transferred from the tray to 8 cm (3 in) pots. Make regular checks on the root growth in the pots by knocking out selected plants when they are about 15 cm (6 in) high. Be sure to water the day before checking, otherwise you could end up with a handful of soil which would mean repotting the plant. If the roots are clearly visible around the outside of the compost, they are ready to

Opposite: *Allwoodii hybrid pink 'Diane'. A very fine deep salmon self.*

Allwoodii hybrid pink 'Doris'. The most popular variety of this group.

be planted out in the garden or potted on for growing in the greenhouse. Keep a careful watch on the plants during this period in case they are unlucky enough to attract some pest or disease. If they do, take the right remedial action detailed in Chapter 5.

VEGETATIVE PROPAGATION

□ LAYERING

Layering is the principal method of propagating border carnations but can be used for other members of the genus *Dianthus*. It is in fact the simplest method for the amateur who wishes to increase his stock of plants, since roots will form at joints or nodes on the stem when they are brought into contact with moist compost. First check that your chosen parent plant is growing strongly, with no sign of disease or insect infestation. It will have at least four to eight shoots, not all of which will be suitable for layering. Reject those which are short or thin as they will not develop into good plants. The best time for layering is mid-summer to early autumn, after the plants have finished flowering.

The soil around the parent plant should be loosened and some soil removed from each area into which you are going to peg the shoots. Replace this soil with a gritty, light sandy compost, a suitable mix being 3 parts sharp sand to 2 parts peat. You will need a razor-sharp knife and pins to hold the layers in position.

Taking care not to snap the stem, grip the shoot firmly in one hand and remove

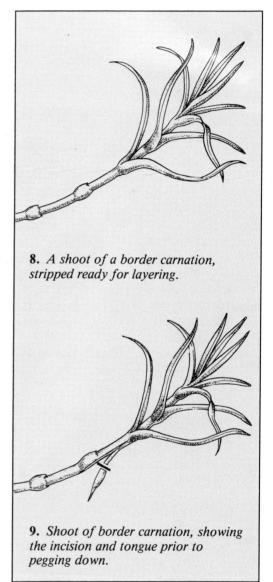

8. *A shoot of a border carnation, stripped ready for layering.*

9. *Shoot of border carnation, showing the incision and tongue prior to pegging down.*

all the lower leaves, leaving not less than five pairs at the top. Select a joint just below the remaining leaves and cut a tongue starting 7 mm (0.25 in) below the joint and finishing the same distance above it. You now have a cut along the stem from which the roots will grow. Now press the shoot carefully into the prepared soil, making sure that the tongue is open and in contact with the soil. Hold it down with a layering pin or a strong hairpin and cover with the prepared compost. As far as possible ensure that the shoot above ground is upright (Figs. 8, 9, 10). Repeat this for all the shoots on one parent plant, level the soil and water with a fine-rosed can. Rooting will take place within four to eight weeks, during which time the soil must be kept moist to encourage root growth. After rooting, the plant should be severed from the parent but left *in situ* for a week before potting up or replanting in the garden.

Border carnations grown in pots are layered in exactly the same way, into the parent plant pot itself. Layering perpetual carnations is more difficult because of the height of suitable shoots above soil level. However, you can then use air layering. This involves fixing a pot of suitable compost at the correct height, generally tied to the parent plant's supporting cane. The procedure is then identical to that detailed above.

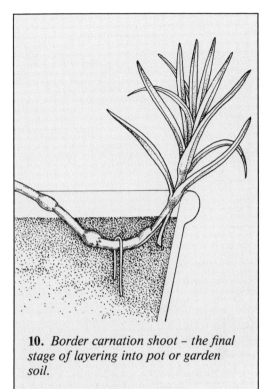

10. *Border carnation shoot – the final stage of layering into pot or garden soil.*

□ CUTTINGS

All carnations and pinks can be propagated by taking cuttings but border carnations are best layered as above, since cuttings often require bottom heat to root effectively.

Perpetual and spray carnations are propagated by simple cuttings from shoots about 10 cm (4 in) long. These should ideally be taken from the middle third of the parent plant, as those at the base of the plant tend to be rather woody and those at the top usually provide the flowering shoots. Some growers designate one plant as a 'mother plant' from which they remove all possible flower buds to encourage the maximum number of good quality shoots for cuttings. Naturally this is only worthwhile if you have a large number of plants and do not mind sacrificing one set of flowers.

The best time of year to start taking cuttings is late summer, as no bottom heat will be required to strike them and they have time to grow into sturdy plants before winter sets in. If bottom heat is

*'Crimson Ace'. A very nice crimson hybrid
pink raised by C. H. Fielder.*

Opposite: *'Kesteven Kirkstead'. An excellent
white ground single pink. Good for showing.*

available cuttings can be taken any time up to early spring.

I recommend taking cuttings from one-year-old plants which have been well watered the previous day, as cuttings taken from dry plants tend to be soft and will not root well. Watering also ensures that the break will be clean when you use the finger and thumb technique as follows. Hold the chosen shoot in one hand at the base of the second node up from the main stem, then hold the upper part of the shoot firmly with the other hand and bend it sideways to ensure a clean snap. If necessary, the cuttings can

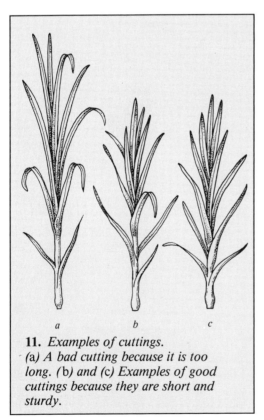

11. *Examples of cuttings.*
(a) A bad cutting because it is too long. (b) and (c) Examples of good cuttings because they are short and sturdy.

be trimmed with a sharp knife close to the node. Never be tempted to pull the cutting away from the plant as this can damage the stem, allowing disease to enter (Fig. 11(*a*)–(*c*)).

It is advisable to get your cuttings into their new compost as soon as possible after taking and preparing them. If for any reason you are not able to proceed immediately, then they should be put straight into a polythene bag, which should be sealed and kept in a cool place, or put into a glass of water as you would a cut flower.

The rooting compost can be made from one of several different recipes. The usual one is a mixture of 2 parts sterilized soil, 1 part coarse sand or fine grit and 1 part peat by volume. If you are not able to obtain sterilized soil, remember to treat the surface of the compost in the tray or pot with benomyl or Cheshunt Compound to prevent damping off and other fungal diseases. Some growers root in pure sand, or a mixture of sand, peat and vermiculite, but it is a matter of personal choice and worth experimenting to find which one you prefer. Should you choose pure sand, you must be watchful and pot on as soon as rooting has taken place, since there is no nutrient value in sand alone and the cuttings will not thrive.

Having taken your cutting, remove the two leaves at the base, dip it in hormone rooting powder, shake off the surplus, and push the cutting 1.25 cm ($\frac{1}{2}$ in) deep into the moist potting compost, making sure that the first pair of leaves is not buried. By pushing the cutting straight into the compost rather than inserting it into a ready-made hole, you avoid introducing air pockets. Set cuttings in trays 5 cm (2 in) apart in all directions, or in pots the same distance apart around the edge. Do not forget to label the cuttings and include the date they were taken, as you will not remember which is which when your enthusiasm gets the better of you. You can always add further cuttings to any spaces in the tray, provided your labelling is adequate.

During the four to five weeks the cuttings take to root, they need to be sprayed twice daily with water at a similar temperature to the compost to avoid dehydration of the leaves. You may be wondering how to tell whether a cutting has rooted, short of digging it up to see! I find that a gentle vertical pull is sufficient. If you experience some resistance to this gentle pressure, you can assume that the cutting has rooted. If it comes out in your hand, put it back and be patient or dispose of it (Fig. 12).

If you are using a propagator, be sure to warm up the compost in the trays for about 24 hours before inserting the cuttings. The temperature required is 13–16°C (55–61°F).

Pinks are also propagated from cuttings in a similar way to perpetual carnations. The best time to take cuttings is in early summer but you can leave it later if you take greater care to prevent dehydration. I consider a dull, damp day is ideal for taking cuttings of pinks, as I have found this gives me better results. A cutting consists of a snapped off stem with five pairs of fully grown leaves. The pair nearest the break is then removed, and if necessary the stem trimmed with a sharp knife. Nine to 12 pink cuttings can be

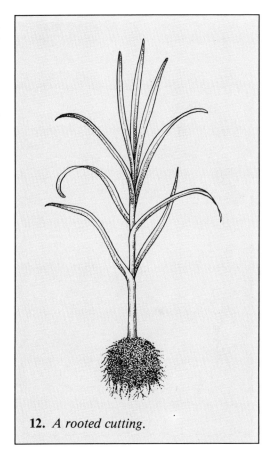

12. *A rooted cutting.*

inserted round the rim of a 8 cm (3 in) pot, or they can be planted in a shady place in the garden where the soil has been prepared by mixing in silver sand and peat. Remember to firm in well and water twice a day. If they are in a pot this can be stood in a cold frame or left outside covered with a plastic dome.

Rooting of pink cuttings will take three to four weeks, after which you will notice that the leaves have taken on a brighter aspect. Once rooted the cuttings in pots should be hardened off by opening up the

'Lincolnshire Poacher'. A good single pink.
It has a lavender pink ground with maroon
eye and is scented.

Opposite: 'Little Jock'. Very popular rock
pink; mauve ground with crimson eye.

cold frame or removing the plastic dome to allow free circulation of air during the day. If the cuttings were taken early they can now be planted straight into the garden in their flowering positions. If taken late, it is better to put them into 8 cm (3 in) pots and keep them in a frame or cold greenhouse over the winter.

There are two further methods of taking cuttings from pinks – pipings and slips (Figs. 13, 14, 15). A piping is the upper part of a young shoot pulled away from the parent plant at about the fourth leaf joint. It should come away at a node and is ready to insert straight into the compost. It need only be planted 1.25 cm (0.5 in) deep. Slips are young shoots pulled straight away from the main stem and have a small woody heel which can be trimmed with a sharp knife if too long. They take much longer to root, sometimes twice as long, being riper, but they are less liable to suffer from damping off, so this is probably the best method for increasing

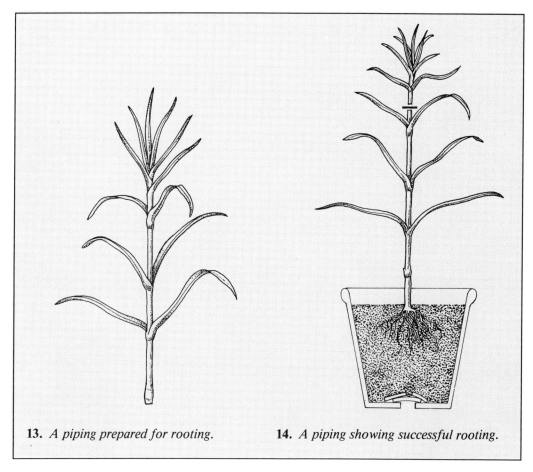

13. *A piping prepared for rooting.*   **14.** *A piping showing successful rooting.*

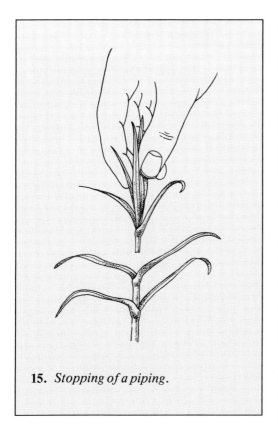

15. *Stopping of a piping.*

your stock of pinks in the open ground. The ground must be prepared and the cuttings inserted 2.5 cm (1 in) deep. Do not forget to label.

☐ ROOT DIVISION

Another method of propagating pinks which was used in cottage gardens in the past was to lift the old plants when they had become shabby and straggly, then pull them apart. They were tidied up and sorted. The best portions, with healthy looking roots attached, were then replanted. This method is not likely to provide the finest blooms but will give an abundance of flowers for cutting. If you wish to try this method, choose early autumn for it, but I really cannot recommend this for present-day cultivated pinks.

HYBRIDIZING

Most named varieties in cultivation today are hybrids, so the technique can be of great interest to amateur growers. Basically it involves choosing two different plants or varieties, taking the pollen from one and applying it to the other. In due course seeds will be produced which, when sown, will have some of the characteristics of both parents, but will be genetically different. These new plants may or, more likely, may not be better in some aspects than their parents. It is quite possible to produce hundreds, or even thousands, of different plants, none of which are worth cultivating, but there is always the odd chance that you will make your name. This outside bet adds spice to an already absorbing hobby. If you wish to try hybridizing this is how to proceed.

☐ SELECTING YOUR PARENT PLANTS

Choose two good, healthy plants, some of whose characteristics you would like to enhance, for instance perfume, colour, non-splitting calyx or strong stem. It is worth noting which of your stock plants produce good plentiful pollen, since pollen production can vary widely and it must be used when fresh, certainly not more than two days old. Designate one plant as the female and the other as the

male. There are no rules to help you choose which should be which.

☐ HOW TO PROCEED

Each flower has two or sometimes three stigmas, which stand out from the centre of a cluster of pollen-bearing anthers. Directly beneath the stigmas, in the centre of the flower, is the ovary, which will ultimately become the seed pod (Fig. 16). As soon as the flowers have developed fully it is advisable to remove some of the petals and all the pollen-bearing anthers from your female plant, leaving the stigmas exposed. This must be done very carefully to avoid damage. The preferred time is early summer when the maximum amount of pollen is available. It is important to pollinate when the stigma is receptive. You can decide when the time has arrived by looking for hairs appearing on the stigma and curling at its tip. As soon as the pollen sacs burst on the male flower, use a child's small paint brush or a torn off piece of blotting paper to transfer the pollen on to the stigmas. Alternatively you can remove a complete anther with its pollen with a pair of tweezers and take this to the stigmas. If you are doing more than one cross you must thoroughly clean the brush and other equipment after each application.

If you have been successful you will notice, between 12 and 36 hours after pollination, that the petals will collapse and begin to wilt. If you have not been successful, there may still be time to try again. After 2 or 3 days remove all the

D. gratianopolitanus *(Cheddar rock pink).*
Makes a good plant for the rockery.

remaining petals and remove the calyx with a sharp knife or your finger nails to expose the seedpod to sunlight and prevent moisture collecting between the bottom of the calyx and the stem, which could cause the seedpod to rot. The seedpod will continue to swell for a few weeks, usually about three, then it will begin to turn brown at the top. When it is completely brown, remove it together with a small piece of stem, and place it in a paper bag or envelope on which you have recorded the names of the parents, date of pollination and any other relevant information. It is a good idea to keep a register of all your crosses, together with the results obtained.

If your chosen plant is pollen shy it can be encouraged to produce more by a starvation diet for about two months, and being kept on the dry side. Take off the terminal bud and leave the side buds to form so that you have one or two extra flowers to work with.

It is important to avoid unwanted cross-pollination. This can be done outdoors by protecting the female flower with a muslin bag during the danger period, and in a greenhouse by covering all apertures with muslin after fumigating, to ensure that you do not have a resident population of flying insects.

The best time to sow the seeds is in midwinter, as both border and perpetual carnations take about eight months from sowing to flowering. Pinks will flower much sooner. Seeds are sown in the normal way as detailed at the beginning of

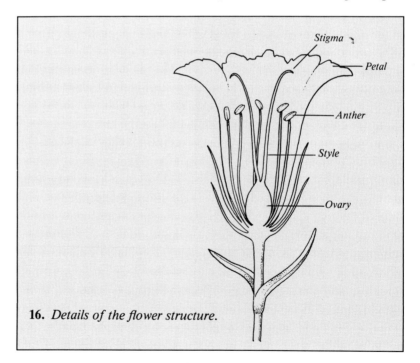

16. *Details of the flower structure.*

this chapter, and will germinate in about 10 days. Those going into the garden must be hardened off. For greenhouse cultivation, pot on into a 10 cm (4 in) pot, in which the plant will flower when the true leaves are 2.5 cm (1 in) long. Do not stop it, then it will go straight up to flower. Now comes decision time. It is only worth keeping those which show any promise, and these should be moved into 15 cm (6 in) pots to see how they progress. Do remember to keep your records up to date.

SPORTS

Like many kinds of plants dianthus species occasionally produce 'sports', which are mutations from the normal appearance of varieties. It is difficult to know whether this should be classed as propagation or cultivation, since you have done nothing to achieve it. However, to save this new form, it must be propagated vegetatively – for border carnations by layering and for all others by taking cuttings from the unusual stem.

If this results in the plants maintaining their new characteristic then it may be possible, if it is as good as its parent, or better, in all other ways, to name it and register it with the R.H.S. and B.N.C.S. The most common change arising from a sport is colour. You will see some notable examples of sports in 'Choosing the Best' (Chapters 3 and 4).

APPENDIX

Those interested in a particular subject
naturally wish to communicate with
others who have similar interests. So it is
with carnation growers. Societies have
been formed throughout the world to
enable interested groups to come
together from time to time to share their
ideas and experiences. The objectives of
these societies, while differing in minor
details, are to encourage the growth and
improvement of carnations and pinks,
and to provide a forum for discussion
and the dissemination of ideas. In
addition they hold exhibitions at various
times during the year to give members
the opportunity to show their choice
blooms.

THE BRITISH NATIONAL SOCIETIES

The first society to be formed was the National Carnation and Picotee Society, which was established in Great Britain in 1877 and concentrated on border carnations and picotees. The latter were much more popular then than they are in the late 20th century. With the continual development of the perpetual carnation, a group of growers, particularly interested in this type of plant, formed the Winter Flowering Carnation Society in 1906, so named to distinguish it from the older society. In due course the name was changed to the Perpetual Flowering Carnation Society and then to the British Carnation Society.

In 1949 at a meeting held in the lecture hall of the Royal Horticultural Society in Westminster, London, it was agreed that the two societies would amalgamate. The combined society was named the British National Carnation Society, known today throughout the world as the B.N.C.S. Later meetings established a council and elected officers, who then formed a number of floral committees. These committees covered border carnations, perpetual carnations and pinks respectively, and each committee consisted of six representatives from the R.H.S. and six representatives from the B.N.C.S. Under an appointed chairman the floral committees formulated rules to govern their particular speciality and these rules, with minor modifications, are still in force today. The new society approached the then Princess Royal, who graciously consented to become the first patron.

Local societies in Great Britain, some of long standing and some specializing in carnations, as well as many carnation societies in other countries, are affiliated to the B.N.C.S. A lively correspondence is carried on between these societies and visits take place.

Unfortunately government regulations have been framed to prevent the spread of disease, which make it very difficult to exchange plants between some countries. It is possible to obtain a certificate attesting the health of the plants but it is very time consuming and the cost involved is high relative to the cost of the plants. There is therefore no free interchange of varieties and we in Great Britain are denied the opportunity of participating in the results of advances made in other countries, as they are denied our new varieties.

Soon after the formation of the B.N.C.S., shows lasting two days were held in June, July and November at the R.H.S. halls in Westminster. The three classes then covered were for the amateur, growers employing gardeners and trade growers. The shows covered border and perpetual carnations and pinks, although the pinks in those days were rather scarce as they had not yet been developed into the splendid plants we see today. The trade exhibitors decorated the walls of the hall with their flowers, which combined with the show bench exhibits, to create a most spectacular display. The trade growers also held a competition between themselves to find the finest box of carnations, which demonstrated the quality of the blooms, the standard of packing and the presentation – all factors important to the wholesale market and the florist.

The shows were discontinued during the Second World War, of course, but were resumed shortly after the cessation of hostilities, though on a much reduced scale. The three major shows in London have been revived, with the November date being replaced by one in October. These shows have increased in popularity and many more entries are now received. The B.N.C.S. has expanded so that in early 1990 it had over one thousand members and forty affiliated societies from Great Britain and the rest of the world.

The policy of the B.N.C.S. is to promote the genus *Dianthus* and to encourage the growth of these delightful flowers. They award medal cards and sometimes cups for the best blooms and best vases of blooms in the different classes in their shows held in London. They give guidance on exhibiting and advice on the registration of new varieties. The border carnation and pinks committees can, after representation, recommend a trial to be held of a new variety at the R.H.S. gardens at Wisley in Surrey, England.

The B.N.C.S. publish a year-book and two news-letters in spring and autumn, which are free to members. They also publish cultural notes on border carnations, perpetual carnations and pinks, respectively, one of which is given free to a new member, while the other two can be purchased at a modest price. Passes for the three London shows are also available free of charge to members. Affiliated societies are entitled to one medal card free and extra ones can be purchased.

Anyone interested in carnations or pinks should consider joining as they will find the society's publications and the help that can be received from existing members invaluable.

EXHIBITING CARNATIONS AND PINKS

Whether you exhibit at the R.H.S. hall in London or at a local show in the village hall, preparations for exhibiting are similar and the results can be just as rewarding. The starting point is always to read the show schedule carefully, noting the classes in which you would like to show. It is surprising how many people arrive at a show with blooms which do not fall into any of the classes specified or with the wrong number of flowers.

When showing pinks the schedules usually state 'as grown', which means that you do not disbud, and more than one flower per stem is in order. If the classification is 'single', it means that each flower is allowed only five petals. The presentation can be improved if a few pieces of the plant foliage are placed in front of the flowers in the vase, making sure that they do not mask the flowers.

When showing border or perpetual carnations the stems must be disbudded where necessary to leave only the main flower. Any support you have used for the calyx on plants prone to splitting must be removed. Again, as with the pinks, some additional foliage in the vase is an advantage. Wiring of flowers is not generally permitted but check your schedule as some societies do allow this. The height of your exhibit, specified by the B.N.C.S., must not be less than 23 cm (9 in) and not more than 46 cm (18 in) from the top of the vase to the top of the tallest flower.

For all members of the genus *Dianthus* it is advisable to immerse half the stem of all kinds of dianthus in water immediately after cutting and allow them to remain there overnight. Transporting your precious flowers to a show may be easy or difficult. If it is within walking distance they can be carried, but if you have to pack them, take great care. You will need a suitable long box, the blooms being protected from damage by using a circular disc you can make from thin cardboard. This disc should be 8–10 cm (3–4 in) in diameter with a 2.5 cm (1 in) diameter hole cut in the centre, so that the stem can pass through up to the calyx. You can support the stems with rolled up newspapers placed just behind the disc.

In addition to your prized exhibits you should take some saturated Oasis for packing into the vases, which are normally provided, a knife and scissors for trimming to the required height, a pen – and don't forget the schedule!

Best of luck! You may end up with the best bloom in the show – if not, don't be disheartened, but try again at the next show.

SPECIALIST GROWERS

Readers who would like to obtain new varieties of carnations or pinks are advised to contact the following specialist growers and raisers:

Woodfield Bros.
'Woodend'
Clifford Chambers
Stratford upon Avon CV37 7DF
(Perpetual flowering carnations)

Steven Bailey Ltd
Sway
Lymington
Hants SO41 6ZA
(Carnations and pinks)

Three Counties Nurseries
Marshwood
Bridport
Dorset DT6 5QJ
(Hybrid and Old-fashioned garden pinks)

Mr S. Hall
43 Larch Road
New Ollerton
Notts NG22 9SX
(Raiser of new Oakwood pink varieties)

INDEX

AUTHOR'S ACKNOWLEDGEMENTS

I wish to thank Bryan and Muriel Carver for help with preparation of the manuscript and my grandaughter, Rachel Furneaux Smith, for the initial line drawings. Also Mr C. Short, Mr C. Stringfellow and Mr C. Sarling for the use of their photographs.

PUBLISHERS' ACKNOWLEDGEMENTS

The publishers are grateful to the following for granting permission to reproduce the following colour photographs:

Harry Smith Horticultural Photographic Collection (pp. 8/9, 16/17, 21, 32/33, 44, 48, 49, 52/53, 56, 57, 60, 61, 65, 69, 72/73, 76, 77, 80, 81, 97, 100/101, 104, 105, 109 & 112); Photos Horticultural Picture Library (pp. 108, 116/117 & 120/121); and Pat Brindley (front and back cover, p. 113).

All the line drawings were drawn by Nils Solberg.